CW00832970

Politics Still Matters

Kevin Dooley

Politics Still Matters

Globalization, Governance, and the Revival of
Regional Minorities

VDM Verlag Dr. Müller

Imprint

Bibliographic information by the German National Library: The German National Library lists this publication at the German National Bibliography; detailed bibliographic information is available on the Internet at http://dnb.d-nb.de.
    Any brand names and product names mentioned in this book are subject to trademark, brand or patent protection and are trademarks or registered trademarks of their respective holders. The use of brand names, product names, common names, trade names, product descriptions etc. even without a particular marking in this works is in no way to be construed to mean that such names may be regarded as unrestricted in respect of trademark and brand protection legislation and could thus be used by anyone.

Cover image: www.purestockx.com

Publisher:
VDM Verlag Dr. Müller Aktiengesellschaft & Co. KG, Dudweiler Landstr. 125 a, 66123 Saarbrücken, Germany,
Phone +49 681 9100-698, Fax +49 681 9100-988,
Email: info@vdm-verlag.de

Copyright © 2008 VDM Verlag Dr. Müller Aktiengesellschaft & Co. KG and licensors
All rights reserved. Saarbrücken 2008

Produced in USA and UK by:
Lightning Source Inc., La Vergne, Tennessee, USA
Lightning Source UK Ltd., Milton Keynes, UK
BookSurge LLC, 5341 Dorchester Road, Suite 16, North Charleston, SC 29418, USA

ISBN: 978-3-639-01764-9

Table of Contents

Acknowledgements

I would like to thank all of the people who have made this book possible. First and foremost, I must thank my loving wife, Lauren. Your constant support has always made my work feel meaningful. You are my life and my soul, without whom I would be lost. Secondly, I must thank my loving family and friends who have always served as my most important sources of happiness, inspiration, and joy. I am so blessed and honored to share life with you.

In addition, I must thank my academic advisors at the Division of Global Affairs, Rutgers University. Professors Alexander J. Motyl, Richard Langhorne, Yale Ferguson, and Alexander Hinton, who aided this project from its humble beginnings and whose support has helped its publication. My years at the Division of Global Affairs were some of my fondest and I owe so much of that to you.

I must also thank my colleagues and friends at Monmouth University; a place that I call home. The inspiration that I receive from the Department of Political Science is overwhelming. Your dedication to teaching, scholarship, and service is truly remarkable. I am humbled to serve as your colleague. Thank you for giving me the inspiration to not only become a better academic, but also a better person.

Lastly, I feel the need to dedicate this book to the memory of my grandfather, Hy Dooley; the person most responsible for my love of politics. Of all the people I have known in life, he has had the greatest impact on me.

Chapter One: Unpacking Globalization, Rethinking Traditional Governance

As the world continues its march toward technological, financial, and linguistic integration certain scholars have argued that globalization is creating a global society that is moving beyond the bounds of traditional governments. They have argued that the technological and economic integration of societies at the macro level is in many ways creating a fragmented society at the micro level. And they have claimed that globalization has the potential to erode the 'traditional' sovereignty of the nation-state and compel individuals to find new allegiances and identities.[1] These scholars have claimed that globalization is an unstoppable force, beyond the scope of typical economic and political behavior. In this sense, globalization has the potential to reach the international system, the nation-state, and the individual; and unite or divide these entities, perpetuating global turbulence and chaos without the traditional means of reinstating order.[2]

In this theoretical arrangement, traditional state-centered identity lacks place and uniformity lacks purpose. Individuals who choose to conform (or not to conform) to a particular system, nation-state, or other group of identifiable individuals have placed the traditional Western notion of nationalism in a state of uncertainty. In an age of globalization, identity, whether it is real or imagined, hemispheric or nationalistic is in a confused state.[3] Ethnic and religious identities appear stronger than ever, while technological resources and new modes of governance have breathed new life into minority communities that several decades ago seemed to be on the verge of extinction.[4]

Minority language revival, a recent cultural phenomenon witnessed in Europe, has been portrayed as a result of the processes of globalization. Scholars like Rosenau and Barber, have suggested that micro-level revival is a response to the fact that globalization is "leveling the cultures" of the world. Rosenau has suggested that globalization (the

---

[1] James Rosenau has suggested that the emergence of advanced information technology has created a potentially, highly educated global populace whose allegiances and identities may shift beyond traditional boundaries toward 'new' frontiers. Rosenau's *Across the Foreign/Domestic Divide*, 1999; and *Turbulence in World Politics: A Time of Continuity and Change*, 1990. Ohmae (*The Borderless World*, 1990) has contended that financial transactions have caused the traditional borders to appear useless and therefore weaken the role of the nation-state in economic issues. Gottlieb ("Nations without States," *Foreign Affairs*, May/June 1994) has suggested that governments would be benefited through the adoption of new strategies when dealing with new or revived identities. Drucker (*Post-Capitalist Society*, 1994) argues that the nation-state is now beginning to face challenges at every level of society, and technology is providing these non-traditional actors with means of support. Held, et al. (*Global Transformations: Politics, Economics, and Culture*, 1999), which defined the term "hyper-globalists" those who see the end of the nation-state, is at hand. Wriston (*The Twilight of Sovereignty: How the Information Revolution is Transforming Our World*, 1997) examines that the nation-state is in a process of transformation, rather than a decline.
[2] Huntington's "Clash of Civilizations," argued that nation-states are a relatively recent phenomenon and only present in "Western" society.
[3] Anderson's "Imagined Communities," addressed the *creation* of national identity.
4 Huntington's "Clash of Civilizations" claims that the rise in fundamentalism around the globe is a reaction to the level of technology present and the rise of Western penetration.
[5] Lundestad in his article, "Why does Globalization encourage fragmentation?" has made a similar argument by proposing that the cultural homogeneity of the world is being challenged by smaller cultures unwilling to conform. Also see Camilleri and Falk's book, *The End of Sovereignty? The Politics of a Shrinking and Fragmenting World*. Camilleri and Falk discuss the economic dependency of the nation-state on the features of technology and financial flows and the ways in which it is attempting to maintain its sovereignty.

process that has witnessed increased information technology, the global liberalized marketplace, the spread of the English language, and the proliferation of non-governmental organizations) has had the effect of creating both cultural homogeneity *and* cultural heterogeneity. In response to this "cultural attack," Rosenau and others have argued that globalization has caused societal fragmentation within the nation-state system, resulting in a cultural backlash and an increased amount of cultural heterogeneity.[5]

When one applies this theory to minority language revival, it appears that these scholars are arguing that globalization, which has already been valued as something that has weakened the sovereignty of the nation-state, has caused the minority language communities to resist the onslaught of global uniformity and therefore reemerge. This however revolves entirely upon theory and ignores the political legislation, namely, recent European-level, state-level and regional-level legislation. In Europe, where language revival is most prevalent, it appears that globalization is not the only factor useful in explaining language revival. Language revival is due to a combination of *both* globalization and the politics of the EU, the nation-state, and the minority group.

The purpose of this book is to demonstrate that globalization is not the only source of minority language revival, but that the governments of the European Union, the nation-states, and the minority communities are also responsible. I will argue that globalization is *not solely* responsible for the high levels of heterogeneity in Europe. Instead I will argue that the *politics* of the European Union and the national and local governments have revived or allowed the revival of minority language communities. Through a survey of the literature concerning nationalism and the conformity or elimination of the minority, the reasons for English language dominance, and the expansion of the European Union, I will establish an argument stating that minority language revival is due to *both* the processes of globalization and the continued presence of nation-states. Therefore, the minority language revival is not just a backlash vs. *McWorld*, but *the result of a variety of political projects with globalization as the background*; furthering the overall notion that *politics still matters*.

Since the project revolves around certain facets of globalization and regional minorities, I will use this introductory chapter to examine much of the existing literature on the aspects of globalization pertinent to the study and how I intend to define the terms 'minority' and 'revival.' Once this has been accomplished, I will present a brief overview of the remaining chapters and demonstrate their usefulness to the thesis.

Globalization

Recent debates on globalization have tended to focus on economic fluidity, cultural homogeneity/heterogeneity, and governmental decline. Scholars tend to be divided as to its definition, newness, and severity. Burbach and Robinson for example, have defined globalization as an "epochal shift" in the concepts of capitalism and liberalism.[6] They have claimed that globalization is a *new* entity that has affected and continues to affect the cultures and economies of the world. They have argued that innovative technology has created a new economic environment, one that has rendered the traditional marketplace impotent.

---

[6] Roger Burbach and William Robinson's "The Fin de Siecle Debate: Globalization as an Epochal Shift," *Science and Society*, Vol.63, No. 1, Spring 1999, pages 10-39.

Glyn and Sutcliffe by contrast, have maintained that globalization is the logical continuation of a process that began with the lowering of tariffs and trade restrictions in the late nineteenth century.[7] These scholars have suggested that the wars and methods of diplomacy conducted by nation-states in the twentieth century had stifled a process that had been created over one hundred years ago. The end of the Cold War and the Soviet burden of communism awakened the 'sleeping giant' defined by them as unbridled capitalism.

In a third attempt at understanding the novelty and scope of globalization stands Anthony Giddens, one who has disagreed with both aforementioned conclusions arguing that globalization is neither a 'novelty' nor a 'continuation.' Giddens has argued that Glyn and Sutcliffe's concept of 'capitalistic continuation' is too difficult to prove because a comparison between late nineteenth and late twentieth century developments has dismissed the notion of the 'novelty' of the present era because of its claim that globalization is "not entirely new." For Giddens, the present era simply constitutes a new wave in the life of economic liberalization.[8] His critique examined the development of the world system not as a fluid, continuous process, but one marked by a period of "stops and starts"; the demise of the Cold War system and emergence of the liberalized marketplace were seen as the most recent wave in the history of economic development.

Yet globalization appears to be more than just economic liberalization. In many ways, globalization refers to a process that is fueled by information technology and free market economics that has resulted in three outcomes: the perpetuation of the global reach of the English language, the increase in the power and number of non-state actors (non-governmental organizations, international governmental organizations, and multinational corporations) and a politically weakened nation-state. For purposes of this book, I will pay special attention to the three following issues associated with globalization: the emergence of English as a global language, the increased volume of information technology, and the rise in foreign direct investment. I have chosen these issues because they allow me to properly demonstrate the concept that "politics still matters" in issues of minority language/cultural revival.

Globalization is a paradox. On the one hand it is defined by economic and cultural homogeneity that has resulted from the expansion of capitalism, free trade, and the erosion of state sovereignty; yet on the other hand, it is said to *cause* greater heterogeneity, difference, and political backlash.[9] As the world has grown into a technologically integrated, English speaking, capitalist system, individuals who had traditionally found great differences with one another are now able to speak to one another in the same language, operate the same technology, and buy and sell goods regardless of their locale. This is the argument that globalization has caused cultural

---

[7] Glyn and Sutcliffe, "Global but Leaderless? The New Capitalist Order," in *The New World Order: The Socialist Register*, edited by Miliband and Panitch, pp. 76-95. Glyn and Sutcliffe can be described as 'transformationists," those who feel that the era of the nation-state is not entirely over, but is in the process of an evolution of governance.

[8] Giddens, *Runaway World: How Globalization is Reshaping Our Lives*, 1999, Chapter One.

[9] Rosenau's concept of *fragmegration* is best suited for this phenomenon. The idea that the world is becoming integrated and fragmented at the same time thus furthers the notion of turbulence. Giddens has also suggested that globalization "squeezes sideways," allowing local cultures to assert their rights in vastly new ways.

homogeneity.[10] What I intend to argue is that the nation-state in an attempt to *maintain sovereignty and distinctiveness*, is creating legislation at both the supranational level and the state level resulting in a European-wide minority language revival. In essence, I will argue that globalization is responsible for cultural homogeneity, but that the nation-state is also partly responsible for the cultural heterogeneity, in the form of legislation that seeks to promote minority language communities.

Information Technology, Financial Development, and Non-state Actors

Information technology (IT), or information communication technology (ICT), can be defined as "computers, software, and telecommunications equipment."[11] Of the changes affecting the world today, Rosenau has suggested that the "technologies associated with the microelectronic revolution that have made social, economic, and political distances so much shorter, the movement of ideas, pictures, currencies, and information so much faster, and the interdependence of people and events so much greater... is *the defining feature of globalization.*"[12] Recent developments in the production of and lowering cost of information technology have created a world in which individuals are able to challenge traditional authority in unprecedented ways.[13] The dominance of the nation-state as the main arbiter of sovereignty in the world is being challenged by the presence of information technology and the ways in which information technology has empowered financial markets and individuals.[14] As a result of this expanded and affordable technology, private financial firms have gained much power in the international community. As Cutler has suggested, "corporations have gained rights through precedent setting cases in North America and Europe where the Canadian Charter of Rights, the American Bill of Rights, and European Union Law are being used to advance corporate rights."[15] Furthering this point, Cutler has added that "the domestic expansion of corporate rights is not being met with a corresponding expansion of state regulation... and in fact, most states are curtailing their corporate control functions in line with the adoption of more laissez-faire and permissive rules that (continue to) encourage corporate investment activities."[16] As a result, economists have witnessed the development of an increasingly homogenized financial market system.

---

[10] Barber's concept of the "leveling of cultures," found in *Jihad vs. McWorld*.

[11] Definition provided by the International Monetary Fund's article, "The Information Technology Revolution," found in *World Economic Outlook*, of October 2001, page 12.

[12] Rosenau's *Turbulence in World Politics: A Theory of Continuity and Change*, page 12.

[13] Friedman's *Longitudes and Attitudes*. From the Prologue, page 2. Friedman discussed 'superempowered' people and the ways information technology can bring people unprecedented political and economic power. Also according to the UN Human Development Report of 2001 entitled, "Making New Technologies Work for Human Development," the cost of new computer storage microchips has been reduced from $5257 in 1970 to $.17 in 1999, page 2.

[14] Friedman, *Longitudes and Attitudes*, page 2.

[15] Cutler's chapter entitled, "Globalization, law, and transnational corporations: a deepening of market discipline," of the book entitled, *Power in the Global Era: Grounding Globalization*, edited by Cohn, McBride, and Wiseman, page 58.

[16] Ibid, page 59. See also, *The Emergence of Private Authority in Global Governance*, edited by Biersteker and Hall, 2003, for an examination of the financial system and the ways in which states have attempted to legally adopt economic principles to affect the open marketplace.

During the Cold War, governmental power had been "based on the ability to tax, the ability to print money, and the ability to borrow."[17] Governments had appeared to be the dominant actors in the world, actors that had at least a certain level of control over profits and taxation. With the collapse of the Soviet Union, scholars have witnessed an increase in market liberalization and, as Barber has suggested, unbridled, predatory capitalism.[18] Governments in this post-Cold War liberalized global marketplace have had a difficult time regulating the activities of corporations. Some scholars have seen the weakening of governmental control as a positive feature, others have appeared more pessimistic.[19]

The weakening of governmental control over economic and technological resources has also witnessed the rise in the number and influence of two interconnected, yet seemingly distinct phenomena: non-governmental organizations (NGOs) and international governmental organizations (IGOs). These organizations range in both size and scope and operate according to their own sets of principles and values. Although certain NGOs (Doctors Without Borders, Human Rights Watch, Amnesty International, etc.) and IGOs (International Monetary Fund, The World Bank, The European Union) were in existence prior to the current era of globalization, it can be argued that their influence on the traditional nation-state system has never been greater.[20] In this era of transnational capital flows and high technology these organizations have begun to operate in conjunction with nation-states, have the power to impose sanctions upon nation-states, and are frequently valued as the "preferred" way of performing services for people in need.[21]

NGOs and IGOs

Since the creation of the International Red Cross in 1865, there has been a prodigious increase in the number of both IGOs and NGOs. For example, in 1909 there were 37 IGOs and 176 NGOs. At the end of the twentieth century that number had

---

[17] *The Economist* quoted Richard O'Brien who is an economist for The Global Business Network. The excerpt comes from the book, *Global Politics in a Changing World*, edited by Mansbach and Rhodes, page 284.

[18] Barber's *Jihad vs. McWorld*.

[19] Much optimism has emerged from those who claim that economic growth and unbridled capitalism are beneficial to the development of the less developed. O'Brien (Mansbach and Rhodes, (ed), 2000, 284) for instance, feels that the globalized marketplace has been a positive development because it "limits the traditional 'abuses' of governments, namely governmental borrowing practices that have historically resulted in inflation. The fact that in today's world foreign direct investment seems to be more prevalent than foreign loans, another optimist such as Dombrowski (Mansbach and Rhodes, 2000, 277) suggests that "this trend could bring capital, technology, and managerial expertise to less-developed areas." Much pessimism has come from Woods (1999), who demonstrated that because of the World Trade Organization, the least developed countries face higher tariffs than developed countries and Norris (2001) who suggested that a digital divide exists within the societies as a result of the growing global inequalities.

[20] NGO's can further be divided into INGOs and traditional NGOs. INGOs refers to international non-governmental organizations such as those that operate across state borders; such as Doctors Without Borders, and Amnesty International.

[21] Edwards and Hulme (1995) in their book, *Beyond the Magic Bullet: Non-governmental Organizations—Performance and Accountability*, have suggested that the rise in the power of NGOs is due to their specialization. In many ways they are better equipped to meet the demands of the people involved because they have been specifically tailored to meet those demands, page 4.

increased 150 times.[22] The increase suggests that the world which at one time had relied heavily on the whims of the nation-states has progressively begun to rely on the presence and support of NGOs and IGOs. In Bangladesh for example, there are currently 20,000 NGOs committed to upholding the human rights and economic security of the people of Bangladesh.[23] Similarly, the European Bureau for Lesser Used Languages (EBLUL) was created as an international organization committed to the preservation of the many minority languages of Europe. Its influence in recent years has led to the passing of international legislation that has held nation-states accountable for their actions against minority groups within their traditional, national borders.[24] NGOs and IGOs have historically had the potential to influence citizens of particular nation-states in ways that seem contrary to traditional governmental proclamations, yet recently this does not appear to be the case. Sassen has concluded that today, NGOs and IGOs are designed as specialized agencies able to properly handle local or national concerns and typically operate in conjunction with national governments.[25] In general, these new sources of power, influence, and identity best describe one of the political sides of globalization.

Rise of the English Language

Globalization is a process that has also witnessed an expansion of the English language. As information technology, non-governmental organizations, and multinational corporations have continued their expansion upon the traditional sovereignty of the nation-state, the English language has emerged as the modern lingua franca of global communication.[25] According to Kemper, "English is currently spoken by 1.2 billion to 1.6 billion people around the world, has a special status in over 70 countries, and is the most widely taught foreign language."[26] Crystal and Pennycook have argued that the English language is essential for one to gain entrance into the global economy.[27] As most Internet websites and financial institutions continue reliance upon the English language, it

---

[22] David Held's, "Democracy and Globalization," a working paper from the Max Planck Institute for the Study of Societies, May 1997. Also, Richard H. Robbins has given the number of INGOs to be 176 in 1909 and 28,900 in Nepal alone in 1993.

[21] From an article in *The Economist* entitled "The other government in Bangladesh," from 1998, was written that there were 20,000 different NGOs within Bangladesh alone.

[22] In terms of the recreation of a European identity, see Soysal's *Limits of Citizenship: Migrants and Postnational Membership in Europe*, 1994. Also Gerard Delanty's, "The Resurgence of the City in Europe? The Spaces of European Citizenship," in Isin's (ed) *Democracy, Citizenship, and the Global City*, pages 79-92, 2000.

[23] Sassen's paper entitled, "The Participation of States and Citizens in Global Governance," *Indiana Journal of Global Legal Studies*, page 8, Winter 2003, Volume 10, Issue 1, pages 5-28. Also *Citizenship and Social Theory*, edited by Bryan S. Turner, 1993. Both works examine the influence and power of NGOs and IGOs in making decisions. Although much of their work concerns countries in the developing world, their analysis concludes that the influence could reach governments at any level of economic development.

[24] Chapter Three of the present work concerns the rise and spread of the English language.

[25] According to Crystal, *English as a Global Language* (2003), in many ways, the English language has become the global lingua franca, a necessary tool for the business world.

[26] Cynthia Kemper's quote from her article entitled, "Sacre Bleu! English as a global lingua franca? Why English is achieving worldwide status," page 41, from *Communication World*, June/July 1999, Volume 16, Issue 6, pp.41-44.

[27] Crystal, *English as a Global Language*, describes the rise of the English language and its necessity to the global marketplace; Alistair Pennycook, *The Cultural Politics of English as a International Language*, claims that there is a strong link between socio-economic growth and the ability of a people to speak the English language.

has become understood that the English language both perpetuates and has been perpetuated by globalization.[28]

The purpose of this book is to argue that globalization through its "leveling of cultures" has led the governments of Europe to pass legislation concerning the protection of regional minority communities in order that they may revive past European cultures and languages. Through an examination of certain European nations, where economic and political privileges of the majority (nation-state) have traditionally denied the linguistic and cultural rights of the minority, I will attempt to show that the cultural homogeneity produced by globalization has led the European Union to pass legislation that promotes minority interests, and thus allows the minority group, a level of autonomy not seen in Europe for centuries.

Minority and Revival

One of the most bothersome features of the term 'minority' is that it lacks an appropriate definition in international legislation. For example, the UN Framework for the Protection of National Minorities does not even define the term 'minority' because as Skutnabb-Kangas has noted, "Only *peoples*, not minorities, have rights according to international law."[29] This is because most of the terminological arguments are based on what is meant by the term 'minority' and what is meant by the term, 'indigenous people.'[30] It has often been noted that there is an ethnic dimension to the term 'indigenous people' and an acceptance of the fact that protective legislation has been based on the grounds of reparation.[31]

For purposes of this study, it is important to demonstrate a greater definition than one that separates the term 'indigenous' from the term 'minority.' I will use the definition of a 'minority' employed by Skutnabb-Kangas and Phillipson in their 1994 work entitled, "Linguistic Human Rights, Past and Present."[32] The authors defined a minority "as a group which is smaller in number than the rest of the population of a state, whose members have ethnic, religious, or linguistic features different from those of the rest of the population, and are guided, if only implicitly, by the will to safeguard their culture, traditions, religion, or language."[33] In short, minority persons must be able to identify themselves as members of the minority community. However, minority membership is often difficult to define because its identity is based upon a culture or language that has a

---

[28] Although certain reports have recently concluded that English is losing some ground in the hypertext world of the Internet, it still constitutes the main language.

[29] Skutnabb-Kangas, *Linguistic Genocide in Education—Or Worldwide Diversity and Human Rights*, page 487.

[30] Ibid, page 487.

[31] Ibid. Gudmundur Alfredsson, in his report in 1990 from the Council of Europe, entitled, "Report on Equality and Non-discrimination: Minority Rights," has been helpful in providing a definition for indigenous peoples. Alfredsson claimed that a group is considered indigenous if they have lived in a particular place since 'time immemorial,' page 5. Also, Cobo (1986) has stated that the indigenous group have 'historical continuity, consider themselves distinct from the group, and are 'non-dominant' actors of the political system.

[32] In Skutnabb-Kangas et.al (eds), *Linguistic Human Rights: Overcoming Linguistic Discrimination*, 1995, pp. 71-110

[33] Ibid, page 107.

limited *market value.*[34] Typically, members of a minority community have had to conform to the standards of the majority for survival. Unfortunately, 'survival' in this sense refers to short-term survival, because conformity to the majority means the eventual extinction of the minority.

Thus, 'minority' is always a relative term, relative to the 'majority. Slovenes in Friuli Venezia-Giulia (Italy) and Carinthia (Austria) are considered minorities because in relation to Italians and Austrians, they are far fewer in number. Yet there has always been another distinction between certain minority groups, one that is based on the presence of a nation-state to which this minority group shares an ethnic, religious, or linguistic bond. Slovenes in Italy and Austria believe they share an ethnic connection with the 'majority' in the Republic of Slovenia. Some groups however lack the presence of a nation-state. For purposes of this dissertation minority groups will be treated and examined regardless of whether they possess a recognized "homeland." I do this because this thinking seems compatible with recent European Union legislation and because it is difficult to distinguish the difference between the 'nation' and the term 'minority.'

The terms 'enhancement' and 'revival' are vague and misleading because they lack precision and clarity. For purposes of this book, I will define the term 'revival' as a recognizable improvement in the scope of a particular minority's language and culture. Since language has been defined as one quintessential feature in defining a group, I will primarily use language as the gauge by which I address cultural revival. Regional minority groups are considered 'minorities' because they deviate from widely held notions of culture and language. Therefore, their languages, long referred to as 'dialects,' have been the focus of direct negative legislation and indirect cultural and economic assimilation.[35]

The remainder of the book examines the continued importance that politics plays the revival of the culture/language of the minority community. By examining the rise of the nation-state and the identity of nationalism, the politics of linguistic 'imperialism' of the English language, the importance of American-driven information technology and foreign direct investment, and the politics of the European Union I will argue that politics still matters and that the European nation-state has the ability to enhance groups it had once deemed problematic in the face of the cultural homogeneity produced by globalization. I will now provide a brief chapter-by-chapter overview.

Chapter Two, deals with the increase in both civic and ethnic nationalism, and the ways in which nation-states have historically determined the role of national minorities. The subsequent theoretical analysis focuses on the development of centralized governmental authority and Gellner's creation of a 'high culture' (interaction of the

---

[34] Market value here refers to the level of importance given to the language in the community. The market value refers to the necessity or usefulness of the particular language/culture to economic or political success.

[35] The term 'dialect' as discussed in Chapter 2, has historically been treated as a negative or primitive variation of a 'truer' national language. The idea of 'direct' legislation here refers to the ways governments have legally attempted to erase the culture and language of the minority. 'Indirect' has to do with the ways in which the dominant society-at-large has forced conformity. Both concepts are examined in the following chapter.

school, the workplace, and the church) which has been argued to perpetuate greater nationalist sentiments. The chapter will address certain processes of assimilation and definitions of language and dialect that have fueled separatist and nationalist attitudes. Following an initial overview of some conceptual problems of civic and ethnic nationalism I will argue that 1.) the emergence of the nation-state meant cultural/linguistic assimilation of minorities, who 2.) sometimes resisted and other times acquiesced in the identity of the dominant nation. This chapter is important to the overall argument because it demonstrates that the nation-state has continued to be the final determinant of minority protection. It is only today, however, that its focus has shifted from the suppression of minority languages to their revival.

Chapter Three describes the causes and effects of the rise of the English language. It will be 1.) an exploration of the position of English in the world today, 2.) its impact on national identity and culture, and, 3.) the ways certain governments have attempted to revive past identities in the face of homogeneity.[36] All points are essential to this study because they focus on the ways in which the English language has increased its market value and is now valued as a political enemy of diversity in the world.

Chapter Four examines the recent commitment of the European Union to the enhancement of regional minorities in the face of the globalization of the marketplace and the increased presence of the English language. Proper attention will be placed upon the relationship between technology and foreign direct investment and the ways in which the EU and several of its minority-focused IGOs/NGos, namely the Committee of the Regions (CoR) and the European Bureau for Lesser Used Languages (EBLUL), have created the potential for a re-imagined Europe; one that is multilingual and multicultural, while at the same time unified.

Following these theoretical chapters, the remainder of the book is devoted to case studies that trace the historical development of three minority groups and the ways in which both globalization and politics have impacted their revival. The first case study is devoted to the Slovenes of Friuli Venezia-Giulia (Italy), a group traditionally considered inferior because of their Slavic heritage. The second case study examines the Friulians, also of the Friuli Venezia-Giulia (Italy); a people believed to be ethnically Celtic who for centuries had witnessed their language and cultural beliefs erased by Italian nationalism. The last case study will examine the Rusyns (Ruthenians), an ethnic group originally believed to be of the region known as the Transcarpathian Ukraine (Subcarpathian Rus'), a group whose identity has been splintered throughout Eastern Europe and overwhelmed by both nationalism and communism.

---

[36] Linguistic imperialism refers to the book by Robert Phillipson of the same name.

Chapter Two: Building Nationalism, Creating Differences

Investigations of nationalism and the rise of the nation-state have typically examined its early and therefore pre-democratic causes and effects. In this chapter, I will examine the ways in which nineteenth and twentieth century nation-states have enforced policies of conformity in the presence of democracy. Proper attention will therefore be placed upon the concepts of civic and ethnic nationalism and the utilization of education and capitalism by the nation-state. I will examine the ways in which places of learning, prayer, and work helped to create national language policies and national symbols (Gellner's concept of High Culture) that forced the minority group into either conformity or resistance within nation-states. Because the overall point of the book is to demonstrate the continued relevancy of the nation-state, I will use this chapter as a way of reasserting the point that minority well-being has always been determined by the state.

Civic Nationalism versus Ethnic Nationalism

During the late nineteenth and early twentieth centuries nationalism was perceived as a strong political and cultural determinant of European states. Nation-states that had a 'purer' ethnic composition, i.e. those with fewer national minorities were determined to be more stable and more likely to prosper.[37] For Ernest Gellner, the rise of nationalism in Europe was due to the transition from agrarian-based society to an industrially-based society by means of an uneven diffusion.[38] Thus, during and after the industrial revolution, economic trends had the impact of motivating individuals to participate in national movements because economic development necessitated a certain level of cultural uniformity. For society to move from 'Agraria' through industrialization, the *state* had to provide a standard, based on a common language and a uniform culture, described by Gellner as the *high culture*.[39]

Following this logic, *culture* was therefore defined by the nation-state and perpetuated by the social institutions (school, church, workplace) and the populace at large. 'Culture' is something the people of the state *share* with one another, which is in some way connected to a past, full of traditions, customs, symbols, languages, and to a future. In most of the European nation-states, centers of learning (schools) were also centers of *citizenship*, places where individuals learned how to act in accordance to the rules and mores of the 'nation.'

Because centers of learning were also centers of citizenship, what had developed during most of the twentieth century in democratic nation-states was the concept of "civic nationalism." For decades it had been argued that civic nationalism referred to:

> "...a community where the sovereignty of the people is located in the individual (the citizen) whose national identity is a sense of political community within a demarcated territory defining the social space that houses a culturally homogeneous group. It requires that people and territory must belong together and that the people are in possession of a single political will. There is a government that respects the law, rather

---

[37] Even Gellner had argued that industrial advancement was determined by the creation of a system of uniformity and those societies with the fewest amount of minorities would be the most successful.

[38] Gellner in *Thought and Change* had noted that the move from "Agraria to Industria," prompted the development of nationalism because conformity had meant greater efficiency.

[39] *Nations and Nationalism* from Ernest Gellner. It describes nationalism as a process that has been perpetuated by the state acting in response to economic change.

than existing above the law, which indicates that civic nationalism is complementary to liberal democracy. Being such, civic nationalism as a social movement is said to be more democratic than the population of ethnic nationalism... the mass are more inclined to be incorporated into a high culture (via education), which gives them the same right of political decision as the elite."[40]

This definition makes a distinction between *ethnic* nationalism and *civic* nationalism. It would appear that 'civic' nationalism is possible only in nation-states considered 'liberal' or 'democratic,' and conversely, ethnic nationalism is possible in nation-states considered 'illiberal' or 'authoritarian'. The classic examples of Hitler and Mussolini's respective fascist states have represented the *ethnic* variety of nationalism and the leading liberal democracies of Great Britain or the United States have represented the *civic* variety of nationalism. The dichotomy is based entirely on the legal tendencies of the nation-state. *Civic* nationalism attempts to rest its cohesion upon a set of beliefs based in the spirit of liberalism and democracy while *ethnic* nationalism is viewed as the primordial representation of the group based upon heritage and blood.

Unfortunately, this dichotomy is flawed because of civic nationalism's necessary reliance on ethnic nationalism. To suggest that the development of assimilation processes and democratic institutions logically led to *civic* nationalism is incorrect. If a society has to endure certain democratic tendencies combined with ethnic nationalism to produce a sense of civic nationalism, this is a case of *transformation* not development. Therefore, to separate the two types of nationalism and to make an absolute distinction between pre-democratic and democratic governments in terms of assimilation and nationalism is impossible.

David Brown has suggested that, "The difference between liberal and illiberal manifestations of nationalism cannot be explained by reference to the distinction between its civic and ethnocultural forms."[41] "Liberal" and "illiberal" tendencies of national governments are not positive indicators of the separation of the term nationalism into competing definitions. Civic nationalism is still heavily reliant on not only ethno-cultural nationalism but also a legal system based on equal rights and a common respect for law. Yet the legal system in even the most efficient and strongly balanced democracy had been created by certain elites, and arguably created to benefit the elite classes who are represented as those who are a part of the national culture and tradition of the state.

National Symbols and Social Pressure

Because individuals need to experience their "collective identity," symbols have been created to serve this purpose. John J. Macionis has defined a symbol as "anything that carries a particular meaning recognized by people who share a culture."[42] It is crucial to examine the last part of this sentence: "people who share a culture." According to this definition, only those individuals able to recognize their identity within a group possess the level of awareness to be able to understand a symbol. Anyone removed from this culture is by definition unable to understand the significance of the symbol.

---

[40] Margareta Mary Nikolas' (1999) thesis entitled, "False Opposites in Nationalism: An Examination of the Dichotomy of Civic Nationalism in Modern Europe.
[41] Brown, page 68.
[42] Macionis, *Sociology*, 9th edition, 2002.

This assertion relies on a great deal of common sense. When a motorist in the United States objects to the actions of another motorist, a certain hand gesture is possibly displayed that symbolically represents a certain level of disapproval. To certain villages in sub-Saharan Africa or main land China, this display might have a different connotation or at the very least, no connotation at all. The "culture" in this example is centered on "automobiles" and in particular, a violation of some perceived driving norm or law. This example is a *traditional* symbol because it represents significance to one group, while representing insignificance to another group.

Assimilation and socialization processes are aimed at the creation of psychological connections between individuals of the state with *national* symbols. Because the creation of a united populace is *the* goal of the processes, schools have been centers of major socialization; but so have other centers of union, namely places of worship and places of business. The tie that binds the school, the church, and the workplace together is *repetition* and *perceived necessity*. All three venues are attended on a regular basis and have the societal value of being of ultimate importance.

The school system, the place of worship, and the workplace serve an important function in national assimilation and the maintenance of symbols because they connect the individual to the nation-state. Children enter the public school system; parents possibly attend a religious ceremony on a weekly basis; and most adults go to the place of employment on a daily basis. The children experience the school at both the local level and community level, yet perform the same "duties" as students across the country. The "church-goers" attend a weekly service in their own place of worship yet feel connected to others who attend different places of worship across the country. Finally, individuals who work realize that others are involved in the workforce and they are all contributing to the society in which they all live. These three areas rely on repetition, but they also link the individual living in the local community to the overall national community.

The school system, the place of worship, and the workplace are all areas that *promote* national symbols and *are* national symbols themselves. When American Christian churches sing "God Bless America," and school children "pledge allegiance to the flag" in classrooms across the United States, symbols are binding the individual to the overall group. Even the economic system (capitalism), embraced by most modern, Western nation-states, is based on the individual's self-interest for the betterment and success of the society-at-large, which Gellner says relies on the uniformity of the culture.

Therefore, assimilation processes are only effective in the presence of *available* symbols. Symbols, rituals, traditions, etc., that have been available because they are perpetuated by the educational system, the religious system, and economic system, which in most areas of the world is capitalism. Yet most new immigrants and minority groups lack knowledge of the symbols because they initially lack entrance into the three systems. In theory these minority groups possess "cultural" or "national" symbols from other nation-states or regions. It is only when the minority groups enter the public school system and observe the standards set forth in the business community that assimilation takes place.

Across Europe, where seasonal and permanent immigration has been constant since the 17th century, minority discrimination has been prevalent. Individuals who were by choice or accident distanced from the influence of the nation and therefore the national movement and culture had only a few legitimate options. The minority group could either

14

a.) conform to the dominant culture or b.) maintain its own culture. Individuals who chose alternative educational resources, alternative churches, and alternative economic resources eventually faced social and legal pressure.

Inferiority and Group Discrimination

"In traditional society, the most relevant social identifiers were kinship, peer, gender, socio-economic and, in settled (non-nomadic) communities, territorial groups, the latter coinciding generally with the village."[43] Social and legal discrimination was based on these social identifiers. Thus, there emerged the prevalence and dominance of certain families and, in particular, certain royal families who proscribed a legal code based on patriarchal traditions and religious affiliation.

Modern nation-states need the unification of its borders and its peoples and therefore proscribed legal codes based on its dominant culture. Assimilation processes have traditionally depended on one's psychological connection to the group. Certain groups obviously have an easier time identifying and therefore assimilating to the dominant group. For instance "Ukrainians and Belarussians assimilated easily with Russians, while small Mongoloid groups like Mansi, Nanayans, Eskimoes,... preserve their separate identity and find it more difficult."[44]

Another obstacle facing many minority groups is isolation from their own culture. "In many cases a segment in the process of assimilation is simultaneously rejected by its own group and not yet accepted by the assimilating or dominant group."[45] Many times these minority groups value families who attempt to embrace the assimilating culture's symbols, traditions, rituals, etc as traitors to their own people, thereby adding additional pressure to the psychological struggle towards assimilation.

For Gellner, modernization is the driving force behind nationalism and the desire for national uniformity. However several critics have suggested that modernization not only yields national uniformity but minority discrimination as well. As certain members of the minority group witness benefits of modern life a desire for assimilation occurs. As the attraction leads individuals to make a cost-benefit analysis of their situation, they will leave their traditional way of life, for the life and ways of the dominant group. Examples of agrarian-based farmers having to conform to national standards and economic models for the benefit of their families illustrate the idea of conformity.

Yet quite often those exposed to "modern ways" who have emerged from minority groups deny the dominant culture altogether and thus come to comprise nationalist-separatist movements. In many ways, the Basque and Occitan movements have been motivated by individuals who had not only faced discrimination from the national government, but from their own minority groups as well.[46] As the motivation leads to the minority's belief in the desirability of national separation, the propensity toward revolution or civil war increases. Individuals will only partake in revolutions or

---

[43] From Algis Prazauskas' working paper entitled, "Ethnic Identity, Historical Memory, and Nationalism in Post Soviet States found at http://www.ciaonet.org/wps/pra01/index.html. Accessed on August 16, 2003.
[44] Ibid.
[45] Ibid.
[46] "Clinging to Life" by Valerie Collins found at: http://www.spainview.com/valerieclinging.html. Also Marya Dumont, (1996) "Minority Sociolinguistics in Europe: The Occitan Language vs. the French State" Master of Arts Thesis The University of Chicago.

civil wars when they truly believe that they are the focus of discrimination based on ethnicity, and that they believe that separation is beneficial.

One Nation, One State, One Language

According to Herbert Kelman, individuals demonstrate two types of attachment to the nation-state: sentimental and instrumental.[47] Individuals are "sentimentally" attached to the national system to the extent that they see it as representing them -- as being, in some central way, a reflection and an extension of themselves.[48] Individuals are "instrumentally" attached to the national system to the extent that they see it as an effective vehicle for achieving their own ends and the ends of members of the other systems."[49] Unlike other symbols or sources of unity, national languages have the capacity to thrive despite changing social or national policies. Sentimental or instrumental attachments rely more heavily on national languages than quite possibly any other symbol or unifying vehicle.

At the sentimental level a national language "serves as a major object and symbol of attachment because it links the present with the future and the speaker with people he/she will most likely never meet."[50] Rarely will individuals develop relationships with individuals outside the traditional associations: family, workplace, schools, community, etc. Although the workplace differs from region to region and the school curriculum varies from place to place, the national language does not. It is an institution of unification and the most profound feature of one's culture.

Language also plays an important role for an individual at the instrumental level because "the national language aids in the development of political, economic, and social institutions that serve the entire population."[51] Although this has been greatly contested in recent years, it has been suggested that national languages allow movement and discussion among the different social classes. Those individuals who feel marginalized because of race, religion, or economics feel a sense of belonging to the national institutions and a greater connection with individuals who make up the majority of the state's population.

Still, most minority groups speak languages other than the national language, which over time have become known as "dialects, pidgin languages, regional languages, or indigenous languages."[52] Each of these terms is labeled in reaction to or in the presence of a dominant culture or a national language. For example, Kurdish, a language spoken by those individuals who claim Kurdish ancestry and ethnicity dwelling in Southern Turkey and Northern Iraq, is considered a "regional language" by the governments of Turkey and Iraq, but an "indigenous" and "national" language by the

---

[47] Herbert Kelman's chapter entitled, "Language as an Aid and Barrier to Involvement in the National System," found in Rubin and Jernudd's book, *Can Language Be Planned*, (24-25)
[48] Ibid.
[49] Ibid.
[50] Ibid. pg. 31
[51] Ibid. pg. 32.
[52] Joshua Fishman in his edited book entitled, *Readings in the Sociology of Language*, quoted a 1951 Report of UNESCO Meeting of Specialists entitled, "The Use of Vernacular Langue in Education." Mouton Publishing, The Hague, 1968.

16

Kurds themselves.[53] Yet is the Kurdish language a "national" language or merely a regional one?

According to a 1951 Report of the UNESCO Meeting of Specialists concerning language in education, there are ten types of languages spoken by the world's population.[54] Interestingly enough, however, each delineation appears to be given in relation to other languages; some more dominant than others.

1. Indigenous Language: the language of the people considered to be the original inhabitants of an area.
2. Lingua Franca: a language which is used habitually by people whose mother tongues are different in order to facilitate communication between them.
3. Mother or Native Tongue: the language which a person acquires in early years and which normally becomes his natural instrument of thought and communication.
4. National Language: the language of a political, social, and cultural entity.
5. Official Language: a language used in the business of government—legislative, executive, and judicial.
6. Pidgin: a language which has arisen as a result of control between peoples of language, usually formed with a mixing of the languages.
7. Regional Language: a language which is used as a medium of communication between peoples living within a certain area who have different mother tongues.
8. Second Language: a language acquired by a person in addition to his/her mother tongue.
9. Vernacular language: a language which is the mother tongue of a group that is socially or politically dominated by another group speaking a different language.
10. World Language: a language used over wide areas of the World. [55]

The delineation presented above is an account of the ways in which ethnic or political groups value their own language and the languages with which they come into contact. The Kurdish language, for example, is obviously a vernacular language, valued as such by both Kurds and Turks/Iraqis alike. It also must be considered an indigenous language. However, the major point of contention has to do with the label "national." For the Kurdish language to be considered a "national language" it must be used politically, socially, and culturally. Although many argue that the *political* value of the language is non-existent because it lacks proper legislative representation, it obviously has political capital, because the governments of Iraq and Turkey have historically feared its presence.

---

[53] Amir Hassanpour, article entitled, "The Politics of A-Political Linguistics: Linguists and Linguicide." Dr. Hassanpour is a Kurdish scholar and one to the foremost experts on the sociolinguistics of the Kurdish people.
[54] Fishman, *Readings in the Sociology of Language*, page 132.
[55] Ibid.

The most fascinating term that deals with language policy is the term *dialect*. Individuals have come to regard a dialect as both a form of the official language used in a specific geographic location and one that is secondary to the national language. The idea behind the term *dialect* comes not from the speakers, but from the "other" language community, usually the one in control of the government.

This separation of the term *language* into a common and uncommon variety has created a subconscious disempowerment of the community speaking the dialect. Fishman has suggested that many negative symbols have been associated with the dialect. For example, "If immigrants from region A came to be a large portion of the poor, the disliked, and the illiterate in region B, then their speech variety (Dialect A) will come to stand for much more than geographic origin alone in the minds of the inhabitants of region B, if they marry primarily only each other, engage primarily in their original regional customs, and continue to value only each other's company, they may, in time, come to consider themselves a different society, with goals, beliefs, and traditions of their own."[56] The emphasis must be placed on the connotation placed on the dialect itself. Speakers of the dialect are instantly treated as members of a lower class even if political representation is granted to them. The case studies of Urdu and Hindi speakers in India by Das Gupta and regional minorities in European cities suggest that a cycle of poverty will continue until minority language speakers either assimilate or leave the state altogether.[57]

One can then argue that national governments endorse one or possibly a few official languages because of the belief that the society and future societies will benefit from this endorsement. The practice known as language planning has been the state's attempt at creating citizens and more importantly citizens who are capable of understanding the basis laws of the land. Haugen has defined language planning as, "the activity of preparing a normative orthography, grammar, and dictionary for the guidance of writers and speakers in a non-homogeneous speech community."[58] This definition seeks to explain the coercive tendency of the nation-state and its capacity to create a homogeneous setting out of a seemingly unmanageable heterogeneous society. It also assumes that the "language" is the only symbol capable of making this difficult transition.

Culture refers to behavioral patterns, ethnicity, symbols, tradition, and common language. What is often overlooked while examining language policy is the complexity of the concept of language itself. For many sociolinguists, language is more than just patterns of speech and a way of conveying information; it is also possibly one of the most common identifiers and realistic representatives of culture. According to Ferdinand de Saussure, there is a difference between "langue" and "parole;" the difference being the expression and value of the words.

Ferdinand de Saussure suggested that "parole" is the words themselves, regardless of situational context and "langue" represents the societal representation and meanings

---

[56] Fishman's *The Sociology of Language: An Interdisciplinary Social Science Approach to Language in Society*. Page 16.
[57] Das Gupta's, *Linguistic Studies in Juang, Kharia Thar, Lodha, Mal-Pahariya, Ghatoali, Pahariya. Anthropological Survey of India, Calcutta,*
Roland J. Breton's (1997). *Atlas of the Languages and Ethnic Communities of South Asia.* New Delhi: Sage Publications
[58] Einar Haugen's article, "Language Planning in Modern Norway." Found in *Scandinavian Studies 33*, 1961. Page 69.

that are conveyed by its members. Group identity is necessary for one to fully understand the language. As de Saussure says, "language (langue) is a storehouse filled by the members of a given community through the active use of speaking… language is not complete in any speaker; it exists perfectly only within a collectivity."[59] And the reason that this "collective" environment is "perfect" is because it gives the people a common identity by which they can similarly experience and more importantly similarly *describe* the world around them.

Furthering the notion of "one language, one culture" is the idea of "one language, one economy." When Gellner stated that "Language is more than a tool of culture, it is culture," he referred to not only its impact on the social sphere, but its impact on the economic sphere as well.[60] For Gellner, it was commonality of language that aided in the division of labor and created a market value for language use. Progress and development lent itself to national language policies and the creation of nationalism.

For Gellner, the idea of language as a separate, cultural identifier was impossible. A similar language united those entering into the capitalist system. During the Medieval Period language policies were non-existent because the economic structure of feudalism did not rely on the ability of the population at large to buy and sell and goods. The medieval serf relied on the protection of the lord, who in turn relied on the production of the estate. It was only as a result of the growing middle classes and increase in cities that motivated individuals to speak a common language, or more particularly, "parole," since the collective identity had yet to be formed or realized.

Gellner's "functional language concept" places the burden of nationalism on not only the socio-political machinery but the socio-economic machinery as well. As the national governments of the 17th and 18th centuries were trying to define a "specific territory" it became essential to also establish "able bureaucracies," powerful enough to collect taxes from a seemingly heterogeneous group of strangers. Common language bridged the gap. The governments had become powerful enough to utilize the market system of capitalism and convince *citizens* of the economic importance of a standard language. Hence the standardization attempts in the 17th century of the French language (in France) and the eventual standardization attempts of Italian (in Italy) and German (in Germany) in the 19th century.

For purposes of this dissertation, it is essential to understand not only national culture, but also how national culture was created and by whom. If one-language policies were essential to industrial development, as Gellner has suggested, who were the elites that motivated others in the nation-state to accept the "rules?" In 17th century France, developing a sense of nationalism was obviously a political move created by Louis XIV as a way of gaining both acceptance and political authority.[61] Those who refused to speak standard French, who lived within the territory known as France, were

---

[59] Ferdinand de Saussure's book, *Cours de Linguistique*, underlines the fact that words have more meaning to natural speakers, than people who acquire the language. This book was edited by Bally and Sechehaye, 1983.

[60] Found in Gellner's, *Thought and Change*, pg. 195.

[61] Louis XIV being a very young man when finally taking control of France used his charm and graces to rebuild the honor of the French monarch that his mother and her top advisor Mazarin had tarnished resulting in the First and Second Frondes.

educationally, politically, and economically marginalized.[62] These individuals (who spoke Breton, Occitan, Basque or any number of minority languages) therefore had a very limited chance of maintaining their cultural and linguistic past. Active participation in the process did not necessarily mean they fully believed in the *goals* of the process. Many participated because it provided them with the greatest amount of opportunity. Therefore, only one outcome is logically determined: those involved in the process of nationalism may have been coerced into the understanding of the nation rather than fully accepting that they in fact were all ethnically united. If in fact those who feared exclusion and therefore joined out of fear or promise were coerced into the linguistic revolution what does this say of the terms "revolution" and "nationalism?" My guess is that *coercion* has a great deal to do with not only the development of national language laws/policies but also the overall concept of nationalism.[63]

"Coercion of elites," a topic of great concern in the contemporary literature of constructivism, is of supreme importance to the understanding of not only national languages, but regional minority languages as well. The term "coercion" has come to mean an "initiation of force, fraud, or threat of force against others or their property" or simply, "the use of force to overwhelm the will of another."[64] These definitions apply to incidences concerning crime, extortion, or blackmail; yet seem implausible in discussions of language policies and/or national identity because these seem acceptable to the overwhelming majority of people.

In keeping with the Lockean order of natural rights and the Humean/Benthamite "logic of utility," democratic nation-states actively sought majority (usually overwhelming majority) rights as the cornerstone of representative government. European governments may have lost absolute monarchy, but they gained a representative style of government, based on the logic of natural rights and majority rule. Nineteenth and twentieth century language policies were not given to the people as they had been in the seventeenth and eighteenth centuries; they were presented to the people as something the people had desired. Individuals chose national languages not only because they promised them financial or political benefits, but because it represented progressive democracy.

National symbols therefore must be considered both acts of acceptance and coercion. To suggest that the governments of Europe acted in a tyrannical manner when creating national languages is not a point of speculation. In this context it is at least plausible that Western European governments convinced the populations that it was in their collective best interests (politically, economically) to speak the national language. The people acquiesced because they themselves were now not only subjects of a king, but individual citizens being represented by a parliament, which also conveniently spoke the national language.

Democratic development gave the majority in the society the belief that their laws were just, not because they were "fair in principle" or based on some ethical consideration, but because the greatest number of individuals "representing" them in

---

[62] Durant's volume entitled *The Age of Louis XIV* claims that Louis XIV was actually only one fourth French.

[63] Modeled after Motyl's discussion concerning the weaknesses of many arguments concerning nationalism in his book, *Nations, Empires, Revolutions: Conceptual Limitations and Theoretical Possibilities*.

[64] The new Oxford Dictionary's first two definitions of the term 'coercion.'

government recognized them as being just. Gellner's "industrial thesis, "based on education and language as a rationally motivated choice is not defective, it is merely *insufficient* when explaining the standardization of national languages. His theory works better when one examines the development of regional languages and their importance in the beginning of capitalistic society.

Linguicide

As societies developed and nationalism was creating social and economic barriers throughout the nineteenth and twentieth centuries, individuals were still speaking languages unrecognizable to many people outside of the particular region in which they lived. Majority-based government and society frowned upon these language communities, recently labeled, "Regional Language Minorities," as being "outsiders" and "foreigners," when in fact most "outsiders" had lived within the confines of the nation-state, paid taxes, and many times had family lineages stretching back centuries. Magocsi in his analysis of the regional language minority known as the Carpatho-Rusyns has suggested that this group has a distinct "homeland" but the regional boundaries of its "homeland" spread across the present day boundaries of four contiguous nation-states: Ukraine, Slovakia, Poland, and Romania, and are therefore invalidated.[65] The Basques of Spain and France have also seen a deterioration of their culture through a similar process of nation-state building, national identity, formation, and linguicide.

The term "linguicide," to which I have previously referred, is defined nicely by Amir Hassanpour as the "deliberate killing of a language."[66] Although this definition sounds quite harsh, in actuality its harshness is derivative of the national policy to which Hassanpour refers, namely Turkish language policy. For purposes of this dissertation, I have argued that "harshness" has less to do with type of government and more to do with nationalism and the propagation of national identity. "One of the reasons for linguicide (also known as linguistic genocide) is that it can reduce the number of (potential) nations, meaning peoples who could demand the right to first internal, then external self-determination."[67] France is considered one of the most vibrant democracies on earth, yet even the French constitution seeks to actively promote the use of *standard* French.[68] The French government and obviously the French nationalist majority, who in theory is represented by the French government, have marginalized regions clinging to alternative identities such as Basque, Breton, or Occitan.

Immediately following World War II, the United Nations in 1948 attempted to secure linguistic and cultural rights as part of the document that would eventually be known as the, "International Convention for the Prevention and Punishment of the Crime of Genocide."[69] As Capotorti and Kangas have noted, linguistic, cultural, and physical genocide "were seen as crimes against humanity," but unfortunately, "when the Convention was finally accepted by the General Assembly, Article III, which covered

---

[65] From Magocsi's article entitled, "Mapping Stateless Peoples: The East Slavs of the Carpathians." (1997)
[66] Hassanpour's article entitled, "The Politics of A-political Linguistics: Linguists and Linguicide." (2000)
[67] Skutnabb- Kangas' book entitled, *Linguistic Genocide in Education—Or Worldwide Diversity and Human Rights*, 2000, page 311.
[68] Article 2, Number 2 states that, "The language of the Republic is French."
[69] Skutnabb-Kangas's book, *Linguistic Genocide in Education—Or Worldwide Diversity and Human Rights*, 2000, page 316.

21

linguistic and cultural genocide, was not adopted."[70] Therefore, individual governments were and are allowed to continue the practice of linguicide on the grounds that it protects the "national interest."

So, linguicide is a reality, but governmental support varies from country to country. "An integral element of the policy has been the suppression of academic study of dialects, geography, and history."[71] There are numerous accounts of individuals charged with criminal offenses for speaking a particular language or dialect. In France, "symbolic denouncement" was prevalent throughout most of the twentieth century. Individuals accused of speaking the Breton language were sometimes forced to wear a "container of some drink or piece of iron around the neck 'until they openly' denounced one (another Breton-speaker/nationalist) they considered a comrade."[72] This practice remained in existence throughout the 1950's and was strongly endorsed by many French nationalists.[73]

Welsh and Scottish Gaelic speakers have continually faced discrimination in Scotland and Great Britain. The 1976 Race Relations Act (RRA), whose purpose was racial and minority protection, does not protect autochthonous language groups because they are not considered "racial groups" or even "ethnic minorities."[74] "Section 3(1) of the Act provides that the term '"racial group' means a group of persons defined by reference to color, race, nationality or ethnic or national origins, and references to a person's racial group refer to any racial group into which he falls.'" All of the Act's protections work within this framework of the "racial group," so that to secure the Act's protection any community must necessarily be classified as a "racial group."'"[75] Unprotected individuals seeking employment need to demonstrate that they are in fact worthy of protection from the Race Relations Act. However in doing so, they as individuals may gain "racial minority" status, get a job because of their "status" and begin to face animosity from their own language community (who may not have been successful in proving their minority status) and of course from the dominant majority in the United Kingdom.

In Slovenia, the newest entrant into the European Union, "adequate minority protection is accorded only to the "autochthonous" national minorities, i.e. autochthonous Roma, Hungarians, and Italians. However even autochthonous Roma do not enjoy the same level of minority protection as Hungarian and Italian minorities."[76] Because the term "autochthonous" is defined in the connotative or cultural sense, it only is

---

[70] Capotorti's book, *Study on the Rights of Persons Belonging to Ethnic, Religious, and Linguistic Minorities*, 1979, page 37, and Kangas's book, *Linguistic Genocide in Education—Or Worldwide Diversity and Human Rights*, 2000, page 316.

[71] On page one of Hassanpour's, "The Politics of A-political Linguistics: Linguists and Linguicide." (2000).

[72] From Ni Hon Hunan's paper entitled, "La repression linguistique en France? Jamais entendu parle! The above quote is my own translation from the original French document.

[73] Ibid.

[74] Wilson McLeod's article entitled, "Autochthonous language communities and the Race Relations Act," first published in *Web Journal of Current Legal Issues*, in association with Blackstone Press Ltd, 1998.

[75] Verbatim quote on page 2 of McLeod's article, "Autochthonous language communities and the Race Relations Act." Ibid.

[76] Quote taken verbatim from a May 2003 article entitled, "Minority Protection in Slovenia: General Evaluation," presented by the Mirovni institut—Insitut za sodobne druzbene in politicne studije (The Peace Institute—Institute for Contemporary Social and Political Studies, Ljubljana, Slovenia, pg.1.

constitutionally defined (by Slovenia) in relation to speakers of identifiable nation-states or individuals considered "native" to the state. The government of Slovenia therefore only offers constitutional rights (rights to bilingual administration, education, and parliamentary representation) to Hungarian and Italian minorities while rights are not guaranteed to at least 7,000 Roma and other "non-autochthonous minority groups."[77]

Because the United Nations, the European Union, the European Commission against Racism and Intolerance and many non-governmental organizations dealing with human rights consider linguistic minority protection a priority, the nation-state, the only important actor in the realist's vocabulary, is having its sovereignty challenged. Groups who claim national autonomy are once again challenging the concept of nationalism, the cornerstone of the nation-state itself, but are having greater success because of the growing technological and financial interconnectedness of the world, the rise in the power and number of minority centered international organizations, and in many ways the dominance of the English language and American influence.

The following chapter will address the globalization of the English language and the ways in which it has risen to a position of power and influence that has forced nation-states to reconsider policies concerning national languages, national cultures and minority groups.

---

[77] From the executive summary of *EUmap*, entitled, "Minority Protection in Slovenia, pg. 1. The article also suggests that non-autochthonous Roma are treated worse than autochthonous Roma because they are considered foreigners who happened to migrate to Slovenia from Yugoslavia after Slovene independence.

Chapter Three:

Globalization, the Rise of the English Language and the Weakening of Nationalism

Because the focus of this book is to argue the continued relevancy of the nation-state in the revival of minorities in Europe, it is time to focus attention on the contemporary expansion of American-English culture and language, and the ways in which the powers of globalization have aided its ascent and impact on nations and nationalism. The investigation will focus on the confluence of five major themes: English as the global representation of Gellner's "High Culture" thesis, accessibility and distribution of American-based information technology (IT), the interconnectedness of the global economy, the impact of English as the recognized lingua franca of global affairs, and the impact of the English language upon nations and national identities.

From the Monroe Doctrine to the Bush Doctrine, the United States has often used democracy and freedom to justify its expansion. However, the spread of American cultural and linguistic influence cannot be isolated to the political will of the government of the United States. Liberalism, the ideology of free trade and capitalism, has been just as responsible for the spread of American culture and the desire of others to conform, at least linguistically, to the economic standards of American corporations.

During the early years of the Cold War, the collapse of the various colonial empires created an international system that was both bipolar and increasingly diverse.[78] The United States and the Soviet Union had created their own "spheres of influence" based on their own political-economic identities and were actively pursuing each other's demise. After several decades that consisted of a space race, several wars of containment and expansion, and fears of mutually assured destruction, the Soviet Union collapsed and the bipolar arrangement that had dominated international politics since the end of World War II had ended. In its place was the emergence of a hegemonic arrangement of unprecedented power centered on the lone superpower, the United States. This development ushered in an era of unbridled free trade, a subservience of national political institutions to corporations and terrorists, a rise in accessibility and distribution of information technology, and an increased expansion of the English language.

Globalization, the process that has been used to define the collection of phenomena mentioned above, has been the focus of literary investigations for more than a decade. Because the terms 'interconnectedness' and 'interdependency' have been paramount in most of these investigations, it is essential to understand how information technology has allowed individuals and corporations (with access to IT) to revolutionize the economic flows of the world and the manner in which the English language has grown to epic proportions. Because the United States has fueled most of these advancements, it is understandable that the English language is valued as a necessary commodity, a commodity that has rewritten Gellner's concept of High culture.[79] At the

---

[78] This statement refers to the rise of two "superpowers" as well as the plethora of former colonies, now states participating in international affairs.

[79] Gellner (*Nations and Nationalism, Culture, Identity and Politics*, and *Encounters with Nationalism*) had repeatedly stated that nationalism is linked with the establishment of an educational system focused on the expansion of the "national" language. Owners of the national language were able to fully participate in the economy and were therefore part of a "High Culture deemed worthy of citizenship" If the English language is overpowering the importance of national languages, English speakers are becoming part of a "High Global Culture."

end of this particular section, I will explore the impact of the English language on the nation-state and in particular the concept of national identity.

Gellner's High Culture and the Perpetuation of Uniformity

The confluence of events beginning with the collapse of Soviet communism and the emergence of the United States as the sole hegemon, resulted in the expansion of global liberalization and the emergence of the English language as an example of a global interpretation of Gellner's "High Culture." For Gellner, one's national identity was determined by one's access to certain institutions: the school, the workplace, and the church. In each locale, citizens interact with one another and are able to witness their own sphere of humanity. Gellner's theory is as follows:

At school, children learn intellectual content and human behavior in the presence of adults (teachers) who serve as role models. Each student observes and participates in rituals in the classroom that are "connected" to every other classroom in the nation. The student learns at the local or micro level but follows a general curriculum that connects him/her to every other student in macro level. Language standards force students to learn the traditions of the nation in the same tongue. The language chosen in the classroom eliminates the need for any other language and the student matures with the belief that the national language (his/her language) is superior to all other languages and is more representative of the people.

At the workplace, individuals engage in activities that create both local and national capital. Individuals work locally, but are constantly reminded of their link to the national system. To gain entrance into the local system, individuals speaking other languages learn the national language because it is essential for economic growth. Those who choose to ignore the national language are economically disenfranchised. A standard language therefore creates greater productivity at the local level and allows the worker to feel connected to the national community of workers as well. The workplace therefore, is not only a *local* gathering but also a *national* gathering. The workers participate in a system in which they feel connected at both the local and national level.

At church (or the local place of worship) individuals witness the local community interacting in moral roles that are supposed to reflect the practices of individuals across the nation. The place of worship creates community and is often the forum where national issues are discussed. Because the place of worship is centered upon morality, traditions, and weekly routines, it is a space where individuals regardless of race or class are able to feel a connection with one another. It is also a place where individuals engage in symbolic gestures, (prayers, songs, etc.) which reinforce their well-being and the well-being of others within the nation. National churches perpetuate national superiority because they ask for reflection upon values that *claim* to be universally accepted. In fact, only those principles that are nationally acceptable are promoted in churches. Prayers or meditations based upon 'universal' principles are 'universal' in name only."[80]

Nevertheless, for Gellner, nationalism relies on institutional perpetuation as a response to what he labeled the "uneven diffusion of industrialization."[81] For Gellner, it appears that the 'culture' of a particular society is the basis upon which industrialization

---

[80] Churches in the United States have often served as a place of universal prayer centered upon American values. The values may appear to be universal, but their appearance may only be heard in American churches, which would therefore challenge its claims.

[81] Gellner's, *Thought and Change*, pages 72-74 discuss the uneven diffusion of industrialization.

rests. For a society to modernize, Gellner argued, the government had to create an educational system that could intellectually elevate *all* of its members to a level in which technical, political, and economic participation could be performed. However, because industrialization occurred at different intervals, the uniformity of the schools, financial markets, and churches allowed citizens the opportunity to become "citizens" and therefore, feel "nationalized" possibly before industrialization had reached their local communities. The "uneven diffusion" thesis suggests that language and culture had become elevated to the state or national level. The adoption of one language and one culture (High Culture) assured individuals living an agrarian lifestyle access to the industrial market and allowed them to feel connected to other members of the state regardless of their economic and political affiliations.

In this era of globalization, these institutions perpetuate an ideology of capitalism and the necessity of the English language that exceed the boundaries of the nation-state and the traditional focus of the national language. Thus the institutions continue to engage individuals in a common set of beliefs, but it appears that the set of beliefs has changed. Today, the English language has become a *global* representation of Gellner's "High Culture" thesis. The uneven diffusion of industrialization and wealth has elevated the English language to a level of unprecedented power. English is valued as a necessary feature in determining one's success or failure. It is the basis upon which many individuals find access to the financial and political markets of the world. It is also a prime determinant of where multinational corporations choose to start businesses and locate headquarters. The following section will address the economic and technological side of the English language and argue that the recent increases in information technology and foreign direct investment have further perpetuated the presence and increased value of the English language and its attack on nationalism.

English as a Commodity for Technology and Capital

While it is true that in many places information technology, i.e. Internet access, fax machines, cellular phones, etc., is unavailable to many individuals, and most of the those who do possess access live either in the United States, Europe, or in mega-cities around the world, it is the *corporation* that is leading the charge in research and development—not the state.[82] The current age of globalization and the "uneven diffusion" of information technology is allowing certain corporations the opportunities to gain access to "untapped" markets; however most of these "untapped" markets have realized the importance of the English language.

For one to gain access to information technology, one must first of all live in a state that has businesses capable of building the technology, importing the technology, and in possession of an infrastructure able to maintain the technology.[83] This means that the individuals responsible for the creation, importation, and maintenance of that country's information technology must be in contact with individuals from other countries who are familiar with the technology; i.e. people from places where information

---

[82] Gross, "The Digital Dimension of Development: A Strategic Approach," suggests that private investment will lead to the development, maintenance, and modernization of the information networks of the world, page 6. Also, Saskia Sassen has spoken of "Global Cities," but my reference involves the work of Cynthia Wagner who discusses the "mass centralizations of populations," or "mega cities" that have developed around certain technologies.

[83] From a panel discussion at the Center for Global Change and Governance, a participant from Duke University suggested that 'infrastructure maintenance is everything.'

technology is created, exported, and maintained. Since the recent geographic expansion of information technology emerged within the United States, individuals with immediate access to computer software, computer hardware, Internet capabilities, fax machines, and cellular phones spoke the English language. As this information technology transcended borders, so did the English language.

The globalization of the English language is therefore a phenomenon tied to both capitalism and liberalism. English, unlike any other language, has come to possess a *global market value*. Knowledge of the English language does not only lead to political inclusion, as national languages have always done, it leads to economic prosperity and technological accessibility. Many multinational corporations have chosen to perform their tasks in the English language and locate their facilities amongst English speakers because the commonality of speech is seen as a way of increasing profits and communication. In this "borderless" world, governments have conceded the economic control they had once possessed, and have witnessed an intrusion on their cultures.

The increase in *foreign direct investment* (FDI) is an example of the ways in which the roles of governments in dealing with their economies has changed. Foreign direct investment has overpowered *trade* as the main feature of economic life as is evidenced by the success of Germany, Ireland, and Japan over the past decade. "Japan and Germany (the two most successful export nations in the world) were and still are the foremost beneficiaries of the liberal post-war trade regime, yet their trade performance seems to have been based to a considerable degree on national financial systems…their financial markets were "nationally contained" and "state regulated."[84] They have had considerable success in recent years because they have allowed foreign businesses (mostly American) to directly enter their respective markets.

Ireland, which has been labeled the "Celtic Tiger," has seen an increase in its gross national product as a direct result of its granting of tax incentives for foreign companies, primarily American technology firms.[85] It is also not surprising that many American firms had chosen Ireland (and recently the states of Eastern Europe) because its workforce consisted of English speakers; a fact that has caused other European and Asian companies to examine the growth of the Irish economy, and begin to reexamine their own language policies.[86]

English: The Great Financial Communicator

It is estimated that 1.6 billion people currently use English in some form, and in fact more people speak English as a second language (350 million) than as a primary language.[87] Individuals who are unable to speak to one another in their distinct tongues have found a common communicator in English. International organizations, international businesses, and educated citizens of the world have begun to associate the

---

[84] Zysman (1983), Shonfield (1965), and Ziegler (2000) as quoted in Manow (2001) entitled, "Globalization, Corporate Finance, and Coordinated Capitalism: Pension Finance in Germany and Japan."

[85] Mac Sherry and White's *The Making of the Celtic Tiger: The Inside Story of Ireland's Boom Economy* (2000), Toomey's, *The Celtic Tiger: From the Outside Looking In* (1998), Sweeney's, *The Celtic Tiger: Ireland's continuing Economic Miracle* (2000) have all demonstrated that Ireland's turnaround is a direct result of certain American (Gateway Inc.) and British firms opening up offices and plants around the isle.

[86] Ibid.

[87] Sampat's essay, "Last Words," in *World Watch*, Volume 14, Number 3, May/June 2001, discussed the importance of English as a means of linking cultures through immediate communication, but the inherent problems associated with the symbolic association of "American" with "English."

English language with success in a way reminiscent of the days of the colony: culturally invasive but economically attractive. Bryson has suggested that the English language cannot be considered an *option* for international businesses, but a mandatory feature of the globalized economy. His examples of European owned truck manufacturers (Iveco) and car manufacturers (Volkswagen) currently performing operations in Asia and South America that have made English the official language of their corporations exemplifies the increase.[88]

According to Baker, Resch, Carlisle, and Schmidt, European columnists for the online editions of *Businessweek Magazine*, it is not only top executives or well-traveled intellectuals who see English as a mandatory feature of society; it is every worker in Europe. "These days in formerly national companies such as Renault and BMW, managers, engineers, even leading blue-collar workers are constantly calling and e-mailing colleagues and customers in Europe, the U.S., and Japan. The language usually is English, an industrial tool now as basic as the screwdriver."[89] The ascent of the English language has created a uniformity of global proportions and many companies have begun to enforce their own language policies reminiscent of those created by national governments during the 19th and 20th centuries. "KPMQwest, the pan-European phone company based in the Netherlands, for example, has mandated that all of the company's e-mails be written in English, even communiqués between German engineers."[90] Other European companies have followed suit claiming that the English language will enhance better communication, but more importantly, enhance productivity and therefore economic growth.[91]

Because communication is relevant to everyone, and information technology has connected a great many individuals across the globe, it is interesting to note that roughly 87% of the estimated one billion web pages are written in English.[92] This suggests that economic advantages are not the only relevant feature in gaining access to the World Wide Web. Linguistic and therefore cultural features are just as important. If one has refused to learn English, one is perceived as being doomed to an uninformed, uneducated, and poverty stricken life; characteristics given by Gellner originally utilized by the nation-state in its creation of national identity and civil society.[93]

The Perceived Damage of the English Language to National Identity and the Response of the Nation-State

If national identity has historically been based upon the acceptance of a High Culture and the belief that a uniformity of culture exists throughout the "nation-state," then the American-English language/culture poses a threat to the traditional model of national identity since it has become more accessible and economically relevant than the

---

[88] Bryson recognized that most of the businesses involved in his research existed in countries where English was not even an official language, namely the six members of the European Free Trade Association.

[89] Article from Baker, Resch, Carlisle, and Schmidt entitled, "The Great English Divide," *Businessweek Online.*

[90] Ibid.

[91] Ibid. Daimler Chrysler in Germany provides mandatory English language classes, as do Vivendi Universal and Cap Gemini.

[92] Originally discovered from Antimoon.com, a web-based English language tutorial service whose information came from a Duke University survey of the Internet in 2001-2002. Accessed March 13, 2003.

[93] Gellner suggested that the rise of nationalism resulted from the desire to gain acceptance in the *national* economy by means of a standardization of a language.

once economically relevant national language. However, is the English language culturally invasive? Or has it become so widespread and deeply ingrained in the former British colonies that it is valued as a mere tool of communication within the model of the nation? I will argue in favor of the former, that the English language, like any language, is a symbol of national identity, and is therefore, by definition, culturally invasive. Its widespread use suggests that it is a practical necessity in an era of globalization, but the increased presence of American corporations and information technology continually remind those who have learned English as a second or third language, that its attainment is only economically relevant because it is *symbolic of the United States*. The following section will examine the effects of the English language on national identity and the ways the nation-state is attempting to stop the trend.

To assume that the English language is divorced from the cultures of its primary speakers (United States and Great Britain) on the grounds that it has a diverse multitude of speakers is to make a serious distinction between English and every other language. The national language, the tool that establishes a High Culture within the nation-state performs its unification through the isolation of the "Other." The "Other," the individuals or groups who possess a cultural distinctiveness from the mainstream, are eventually forced (through the system of capitalism) to abandon their own language for the national language/culture, because it is the national language/culture that can ensure their economic and political wellbeing.

Every nation-state that has had a one-language policy has witnessed this trend. In France, the outlawing of the Breton language by governmental decree reduced the number of Breton speakers, yet the economic and political isolation caused by one's refusal to learn standard French was even more severe. Economic and political incentives propelled nationalism within the nation-state. In today's world of cross-border transactions, multinational corporations, and information technology, the English language has the potential to erode the traditional definition of nationalism and national identity.

If one examines the spread of the English language, one will discover that the English language is in its current position because of what Phillipson has described as a history of "linguistic imperialism."[94] The rise of the English language is a narrative based upon linguistic intrusion and cultural superiority. Its colonial experience was dependent upon its language and culture, both of which were utilized for economic gain and political control, and its current dominance is due to its overwhelming presence in business and information technology.

The English language has become the recognized *lingua franca* because it appears to represent opportunity. In a world of business and technology, those able to speak the language of capitalism will have a greater opportunity for success than those that are unable to speak English.[95] This has and will continue to cause an uneven diffusion of technology; a phrase reminiscent of Gellner's concept. However, this 'uneven diffusion'

---

[94] Robert Phillipson's *Lingusitic Imperialism*, Oxford University Press, 1992.
[95] In his book, *The Future of English?*, Graddol has suggested that the English language is so entrenched in the economic culture of capitalism that its replacement as lingua franca, must come from a source of greater population and higher technology.

29

appears to be unregulated.[96] The government of the United States is not driving the 'uneven diffusion' of technology and opportunity. The multinational corporations of the United States appear to be the ones responsible for the increased value attributed to the English language.

Because capitalism 1.) thrives on profit and efficiency and 2.) furthers the 'uneven diffusion' of resources, the nation-state has the potential to lose its most distinguishing characteristic: its national identity. If the English language is currently recognized as the global lingua franca and globalization is increasing cross-border transactions than it is possible that English will eventually replace the *national* language as the most common first language most countries. This has significant implications for the governments of the world.

Proclamations that ban or outlaw the English language could prove to be financially ruinous for a country. If the number of English speakers in a particular state is a major incentive for foreign investment, than a language ban could seriously hinder the economic development of that particular country and possibly lead to immigration or even worse, revolution. In either case the net loss (financial or human) perceived by the government far outweighs the damage such a proclamation could cause.

Another serious implication for the nation-state is the loss of national identity. Individuals who for centuries have engaged in specific rituals, based on a common language, and have experienced traditions as an imagined community, will feel the divisiveness of the English language. The 'uneven diffusion of industry,' which had initially perpetuated the need for a High Culture, which was motivated in the school, the workplace, and the church, has produced a similar need for the English language.

It has been this logic that has caused certain critics to claim that the nation-state is "withering away," and the Westphalian order is "ending." However I am not as certain. The world of nation-states and national identities are still very much a part of the landscape of politics; however, in recent years they have had to *share* some of their power with a host of other actors, whose interests at times strongly diverge from traditional, *national* ambitions, and other times have replaced some of the functions of national governments.[97] Non-governmental organizations (NGO's) and transnational corporations (TNC's), some benevolent others tyrannical, are simultaneously marching on the territory once deemed to be of ultimate importance in global affairs, but the nation-state in response to these processes has attempted to maintain sovereignty through initiatives that involve the revitalization of its non-American identity.

Throughout the world, school children are attempting to balance the national with the global, their nationalism in the presence of the English language. Workers have begun to communicate in the world of international business in the language that is common to all speakers. Yet how have the governments reacted to the dominance of the English language? Although the English language has transcended the traditional borders of the nation-state, it has been the nation-states that have created policies that have reflected a

---

[96] The themes of economic liberalization found in the works of Cutler, Strange, and Biersteker and Hall all suggest that the end of the Soviet Union opened up markets and transnational flows moved faster than national governments.

[97] Cutler, Haufler, and Porter's (eds) book entitled, *Private Authority and International Affairs*, and in particular their chapter (12) entitled, "The Contours and Significance of Private Authority in International Affairs," discusses the fact that many multi-national corporations have begun to change the ways in which citizens interact with their governments.

desire to maintain their national sovereignty, thus suggesting that their existence still matters.

In India for example, there exists a cultural divide directly related to the presence of the English language. Salmon Rushdie commenting on contemporary Indian society has suggested, "The children of independent India seem not to think of English as being irredeemably tainted by its colonial provenance, ...(but) use it as an Indian language, as one of the tools they have to hand."[98] Rushdie's comment argues that the English language is not viewed as a cultural problem in India. Yet, when one examines the government policy in India, one must wonder why the name of Calcutta has been changed back to its Hindi name Kolkotta, and Bombay changed to Mombai. If the government and people of India were as comfortable with the English language as Rushdie has claimed, then the need for a name change would never have been addressed.

Japan, a country whose economy has historically been stronger in comparison to other Asian countries, has witnessed, "criticism directed at an increasing number of foreign (English) words that are expressed in kakama forms (Japanese), such as 'deribari,' the slang word that means 'delivery' and 'akusesu' the word used to express 'access'... This bastardization has prompted the National Institute for Japanese Language to propose translated terms for such words like "gaibu itaka' for 'autososhingu' (a borrowed word from English that means 'outsourcing'), a kakama word used by the Japanese."[99] The Japanese government has determined that the entrance of English words into their lexicon have become more than just tools for communication, they have become symbolic of an invasive culture.

In Korea a different approach to the English language has been conceived, one based on the combination of English language and Korean identity. This incredible paradox is being witnessed in the Korean Minjok Leadership Academy, an academy of advanced students who are simultaneously taught the English language through a prism of Korean nationalism.[100] Many Asian countries have begun to "view globalization from an instrumentalist approach...treating globalization as a means to achieve a competitive edge for the nation.[101] This theory is based solely on the economic significance of the English language, and not its cultural dynamics. This is an interesting phenomenon that has begun to culturally challenge the concept of the nation-state because it both expands and refutes Gellner's thesis.

If national identity is not only an "imagined community' but also one that was devised and accepted on the basis of economic and social inclusion, who is to say that its existence is permanent? If the English language continues to expand exponentially through the growing number of American investments and IT resources, the American-English hegemony will continue to attract an immeasurable amount of both love and hate. Yet it appears that even devotion to the English language is based on the separation of language and culture. Although many people in Asia value the importance of English, the governments have made a decision about its power and influence. They obviously deem the English language as a threat to Indian, Japanese, or Korean national identity. The

---

[98] The quote of Rushdie comes from Crystal, *English as a Global Language*, page 184.

[99] Matsuzawa, "New Dictionary for New Times," *The Yomiuri Shimbun*, September 30, 2003.

[100] Working paper of Gi-Wook Shin entitled, "The Paradox of Korean Globalization," from the Asia/Pacific Research Center at Stanford University, January 2003.

[101] Ibid.

strong promotion of Korean national identity is testimony to the fact that the nation-state fears the loss of its people and presumed authority.

Globalization is the force that has driven both the embrace of and rejection of American English. Although I have briefly used Asian examples as exemplary of this new social/economic/political relationship between language and national identity and their relationship with American-English and culture, I will continue this exploration with Europe as the focus of further investigation and will explore the revival of regional minorities across Europe as a result of EU legislation and the globalization of the English language.[102] In particular, I will be exploring the relationship between European governmental and non-governmental organizations and the way that globalization in conjunction with the legislation of the European Union has given regional minorities, those groups once marginalized by national governments, to reemerge socially, politically and economically.

---

[102] Europe was chosen because it represents the model of the nation-state presented in the previous chapter.

Chapter 4: Globalization and Governance (Not Just Globalization)

In recent years a great deal of literature has been focused on the belief that in certain ways the nation-state has lost part of its sovereignty due to the processes of globalization. The literature tends to address issues of private authority, terrorism, capitalism, information technology, and the multitude and strength of certain non-governmental organizations in a turbulent and fast-paced world. According to this logic, the revival of regional minority languages would result from the processes of globalization. The following chapter will argue that globalization is not the only reason for the revival of minority groups. I will argue that the empowerment and revival of European regional minorities is due to the rise of certain minority centered institutions, technological resources, and educational programs of the European Union. Because the final three chapters deal with particular case studies of European minorities, the purpose of the following chapter is to demonstrate the critical role that the European Union is playing in the enhancement of regional minorities in the face of American-English laden information technology.

As the English language continues to dominate the cultures and languages of Europe through the processes of globalization, it has been the European Union that has attempted to safeguard European culture as a whole. The creation of the Committee of the Regions (CoR), created by the Maastricht Treaty, designed to "give an advisory role to subnational autonomous regions such as Scotland and Wales in the United Kingdom, Catalonia in Spain, and the Lander in the German Federal Republic was established in response to a growing demand for greater regional autonomy and a corresponding belief that, as regions grow in self-governing capacity, they too should have a voice in the EU."[103] For the regional minority communities, as well as the governments of Europe, it is believed that the language of that voice is increasingly becoming English.

Just as the intelligentsia of past European societies had turned to the Latin language for its communication with the outside world, regional minorities have discovered that their support comes from knowledge of the English language.[104] What is of importance to this work however, is the fact that the English language has a disunited common enemy: the EU international governmental and cooperating non-governmental organizations and the nation-states of Europe. They both oppose the power and influence of the English language. Both the nation-states of Europe and the institutions of the European Union view the English language as a threat to national sovereignty and diversity. The position of the EU concerning human rights and diversity in many ways contradicts a European society that is becoming more influenced by the English language. This is the reason that the EU and the nation-states of Europe have helped fund initiatives that deal with minority protection and linguistic revival.[105]

As Chapter 2 had discussed, the nation-states of Europe, reliant upon unity and standardization, had always felt it necessary to safeguard their interests through the adoption of constitutional articles that pertained to their respective national languages.

---

[103] Wood and Yesilada's, *The Emerging European Union*, Third Edition, page 109.

[104] This reference comes from Magocsi (1979) who stated that many of the intelligentsia of the Subcarpathian Rusyns had communicated in the 19th century through Latin, to gain a voice for their people.

[105] Magocsi has argued that minority revival emerges from the minority group itself. I am exploring the possibility that transnationalism overpowers national sovereignty and allows groups to reinvest in their past glory.

This was in response to the concern that dissident views, dissident languages, and dissident cultures were all contrary to the views, language, and culture of the nation-state. It was believed that political strength, economic well-being, and educational development resulted from the unified beliefs of the "nation."

Although national-separatist movements have been common in certain areas of Europe for centuries, rarely have these groups attempted to gain a degree of autonomy through peaceful measures. Most have relied upon the belief that national separation (obviously endorsed by the opposing nation-states) justifies violent reaction to the nation-state. Terrorist activities had been labeled "acts of freedom" by the perpetrators in their hopes of gaining autonomy. Recently however, regional minorities have been given certain protections by the EU and have gained minimal access to information technology and have therefore in many ways forced the nation-state to acknowledge minority culture and status in the face of American English.

Following World War II there was a trend in Europe, especially in areas that had been dominated by fascism, to create governments that were politically decentralized. In Germany the "Lander" had been created as a direct response to a tendency of political centralization and eventual authoritarianism, and in Italy, a unitary system of rule was created, however, autonomous regions were mandated to curb the type of xenophobia that had occurred during the reign of Mussolini. According to most of the constitutions of the countries of Europe a provision is made that allows minority rights and provisions. This law however has rarely been enforced.

Article 6 of the 1947 Italian constitution mandated that the regional languages of Italy (a list of these languages was developed in 1985) be protected. It was not until the passage of Language Law 482 in 1999, that action and enforcement actually began; a language law valued by many that was designed in response to the growing pressure of both the EU agencies and the European Bureau for Lesser Used Languages.[106] The Italian government is not alone however in its hesitant stance toward minority groups. France, as recently as 1995 had reaffirmed its constitutional decree that stated that standard French is the only language of the "nation."[107] Public funding for minority cultural or linguistic endeavors has rarely ever occurred.

Since the middle of the 1990s, minority groups that been privileged to see at least some growth and protection because of the European Bureau for Lesser Used Languages (EBLUL) and the European Commission's Committee on Culture and Education. Local leaders have been able to circumvent national legislation and formulate a claim that deals with their respective right to speak a certain language based on the reinterpretation of human rights to include linguistic rights as part of its tenets. The European Parliament in December 2002 "earmarked 1.000.000 euros for regional and minority languages,

---

[106] Language Law 482/1999 was designed to enhance the recognized minority language communities in Friuli Venezia-Giulia. It in many ways had been based on the recommendations of the EU Commission , the local department of the EBLUL, and the Framework Convention for the Protection of National Minorities. Eurolang, through its website has continually issued statements that have raised minority issues to the global stage.

[107] Although the Deixonne Act of 1951 allowed four minority languages the right to provide students in several minority dominated regions, very few francs had been spent on the policy.

dialects, and cultures in Budget Line B3-1000 for 2003."[108] The European Parliament has also assisted in the "development of the Joint Internet Portal to European Regional and Minority Languages with the Mercator Centers" to ensure better access and technological infrastructure to individuals living in minority areas that have typically been economically disadvantaged, i.e. the Slovenes in Carinthia, Austria; the Slovenes in city of Udine, Italy; etc. To better understand the revival of European regional minorities I will now exaine the development of the different cooperative non-governmental organizations of the European Union.

Non-Governmental Organizations, Corporations, Education, and the Revival of the Region.

When the Federal Union of European Nationalities was created in 1949 its viability was questionable at best. The European continent had laid witness to the destructive nature of two wars, an attempted extermination of an entire race brought about by the extremes of unbridled nationalism, and deep economic suffering. Regional revival was not perceived as a priority. European heads of state were more consumed by reconstruction and conflict resolution and prevention than with the extension of rights to local cultures.

The terms "regional" or "indigenous" were years away from acceptance. The European Coal and Steel Community, Euratom, and the European Economic Community, the earliest institutions of the European Community were emerging as organizations committed to economic revitalization and integration. Unity was understood as a way the nation-states of Europe could emerge as a liberal, unified body where economic growth could extend across the continent, until finally a transnational government could regulate the actions of all actors. As Calleo has suggested, the process of "integration in one economic sector was expected to 'spill over' to others…as member states opened and integrated their economies, their disputes would gravitate toward Brussels for settlement… (and eventually) interest groups and politics would refocus on the European level, and ultimately, sovereignty itself would migrate to that level."[109] However, the initial structure "came into existence in the 1950's as the initiatives of statesmen like Schuman and Spaak and major national leaders like Adenauer and de Gasperi."[110] The attention of the 'new' Europe was focused on rebuilding the national governmental structure in an international setting, not Spinelli's view of a "federal superstate" or Brugmans' 'personalist' view of Europe, one of autonomous regions, local communities, and corporatist associations."[111]

Following World War II and throughout most of the Cold War, there was a prevailing concern that regional minorities, those that represented local or "sub-nationalist" interests were impediments to the wellbeing and security of the European nation-state and the emerging European Community. Breton involvement with the Nazi party during World War II, assassinations and assassination attempts perpetrated by

---

[108] From The EBLUL, Annex A.2: Introduction to the Draft Work Programme 03-04, page 1. Accessed from http://ww2.eblul.org:8080/eblul/Public/projets_en_cours/priorities_and_resul8772/view . Found on February 26, 2004.
[109] Verbatim from Calleo's, *Rethinking Europe's Future*, page 137.
[110] Ibid.
[111] Calleo mentions (page 137) Spinelli and Brugmanns as representative of the two views of Europe in the 1950's that were resoundingly opposed by other statesmen. Interestingly enough, it is the views of Brugmanns and Spinelli that seem to be most reflective of the post Maastricht EU.

Basque nationalists in Franco's Spain, and car, bus, or restaurant bombings carried out by members of the Provisional Irish Republican Army in London and Northern Ireland furthered a hostile attitude toward regional minorities as a whole.[112] The EC of the 1960's and 1970's valued transnational or local organizations committed to minority preservation as an organization representative of a people not worthy of representation.[113] This fact resulted in the almost invisible international presence of the Federal Union of European Nationalities during much of the Cold War.

The terms by which the FUEN was created established a strong commitment toward its central belief of peaceful resolution, and an agenda free from territorial expansion and secession.[114] Often minority movements resisted active involvement with the FUEN because many minority groups felt that the beliefs of the FUEN had been authored by and tailored to the whims of the nation-states of Europe or that the collective interests of the 'many regions' would neglect individual interests[115] The FUEN was and still is a *non*-governmental organization, but it had always operated in close conjunction with the institutions of the EC at a time when commitment to regional development was at a minimum. Nevertheless, the FUEN remains the oldest transnational European minority-based NGO and its working papers and congresses have played an advisory role in the ratification of the European Charter for Regional Minorities and the Framework Convention on the Protection of National Minorities.

Yet in many ways, it can be argued that the Federal Union of European Nationalities would not have had a tremendous impact on the lives of minorities had it not been for the rise of the American IT industry in Europe and the merging interests of NGOs and European multinational technology based corporations. This *merger* was responsible for the minorities of Europe in becoming a commodity; one in which both the corporations and the NGOs could succeed.

In 1982, as a result of the Arfe Resolution of the European Parliament, the European Bureau for Lesser Used Languages was established as a non-governmental organization committed to the protection of the speakers of indigenous languages and their respective communities across Europe.[116] The EBLUL claims to be the "protector of

---

[112] For the most recent and best analysis of European "regional" terrorism's past and present there is the International Institute for Strategic Studies' book entitled, *The Military Balance, 2002-2003*. It provides a regional approach to the ways in which regional groups have perpetrated acts against the innocent and the government with special European focus on the Basque's ETA, and the Provisional Irish Republican Army. Another recent book on European terrorism is Zulaika and Douglass's *Terror and Taboo: The Follies, Fables, and Faces of Terrorism*, 1996. This book focuses on the historical prejudices and resulting violence based on the European brand of separatist terrorism.

[113] The organization to "deal" with terrorism was known as the TREVI group and it was created in 1975. The group's purpose was to prevent terrorism across the EC, however as Messina and Thoriez (2002) have suggested, it focused primarily on non-EC terrorism. The regionally based European separatist groups were to be determined by the national authorities of each country, and the policies typically punished all those identified as either Basque or Irish Catholic as enemies of the state.

[114] Keating (2002) has suggested that the FUEN was created as a way the nation-states could appear to be on "good terms" with separatist groups. However, it was specifically designed to 'contain' the minority groups through its policy of non-expansion, chapter one. The FUEN has historically been denied a great deal of authority because its seven-member, elected group of officials is made up of minority group leaders, who have been often blamed for terrorist activities.

[115] Ibid.

[116] From the homepage of the European Bureau of Lesser Used Languages (www.eblul.org) found at the "About Us" page.

the 40 language communities of Europe" through its dissemination of resolutions passed by the EU institutions to the local regions, its maintenance of Eurolang, the news agency for European regional minorities, and its advisory role in major governmental organizations like the European Parliament, the Council of Europe, and the United Nations Economic and Social Council" it appears to have more of an impact on the everyday lives of the regional minorities than the FUEN.[117] Although the EBLUL receives funding from 14 member state committees (MSCs), the European Commission (budget allocated for culture and education) several regional parliaments, and is "legally established" under Irish and Belgian law, its power and success in recent years seems to have emerged from its association with information technology, certain IT corporation, educational initiatives, and new media outlets.[118]

The European Bureau for Lesser Used Languages operates as the axis upon which minority protection revolves. EBLUL member state committees act independently of their respective nation-states and report exclusively to the EBLUL on issues that affect their respective regional minorities. Although this appears to be a more traditional exercise in information gathering, the EBLUL has also begun to utilize and strengthen its presence in the World Wide Web.

Eurolang created by the EBLUL, is the recognized news agency for minority linguistic groups across Europe, and has a web site which documents and reports detailed accounts of minority treatment and legislation.[119] Created in 1991 as the Eurolang Project, it wsa initially devised as a way of aiding government translation in a linguistically diverse Europe. Because the creation of the European Union meant the integration and assimilation of countless government documents written in numerous foreign tongues, the Eurolang Project imagined a consortium of high tech producers and academics that would be able to enhance the productivity of the bureaucracy.[120]

In addition to Eurolang, the EBLUL has utilized the work of Mercator Education and SOCRATES, two European Commission funded enterprises committed to the creation of better educational facilities for the people of Europe. This is of great significance because both Mercator Education and SOCRATES have recently created certain educational projects committed to the advancement and protection of minority education.[121] Lingualia.net, the name given to the project created by Mercator Education, and LINGUA, one aspect of the SOCRATES initiative, both focus on the implementation of minority educational resources and facilities.

---

[117] Ibid.

[118] The information concerning Ireland and Belgium's legal recognition of the organization emerges from the EBLUL's homepage as mentioned in the previous footnote. However the comment that refers to its association with the IT community is part of my own investigation.

[119] Eurolang.net

[120] SITE, a French IT corporation completed the terms of the project in 1991, and created consortium of corporations and academics committed to European translation. The corporate participants were: Cap Gemini Innovation, Simens Nixdorf, Krupp Industries, and Lexicon. The academic participants were: the Universities of Wales, Essex, Salemo, Pisa, Barcelona, and Torino. Found in an article entitled, "Presentation of the Eurolang Project," written by Seite, Bachut, Maret, and Roudaud at SITE in France. From Proc. Of Coling-92, Nantes, August 23-28, 1992.

[121] According to *The Magazine*, Issue 22, the cultural and educational journal of the European Commission, SOCRATES has been given permission to ensure that European children speak numerous languages. In areas where minority languages are particularly strong, the course of action has been to advance the idea of learning the local and the national language.

Lingualia.net was created for the enhancement of minority languages and is accessed exclusively through the World Wide Web. The website acts as a search engine, an encyclopedia, a "chatroom," and a place where academics, poets, writers, and anyone interested in the understanding of a particular minority language or language community can assemble to find or leave information.[122] Lingualia.net is of significance to this particular study for two reasons: first, it demonstrates that the European Commission not only values the work of the EBLUL, but that it values it enough to provide funding for an educational initiative dealing with minority groups, and second, Mercator Education is willing to place this investment in an *online* resource, when many have argued that local communities by their very nature, lack the educational structure and accessibility to computers. Lingualia.net *relies* upon the electronic medium. This reliance suggests that the European Union is confident that its member states and future member states will not only possess the necessary technical infrastructure, but also that its regional minorities will have access to it as well.

In conjunction with Lingualia.net, the European Commission's committee on Education and Training has created a program entitled SOCRATES whose goal is to strengthen education at all levels within the EU and to ultimately, create an accepted multilingual society. SOCRATES, whose components are COMENIUS, ERASMUS, GRUNDTVIG, LINGUA, and MINERVA, has worked to unite schools and curricula across Europe in ways that focus on social and cultural unification. Because understanding different cultures is believed to be of utmost importance to the European Commission, the European Union has authorized LINGUA (beginning in 1990) to create European-level guidelines for multilingual education.[123] Although European universities continue to be *nationally* oriented, the European Union has decided to create language diversity at the primary and secondary levels of education in an attempt to maintain European culture. The rationale behind LINGUA is demonstrated in three interrelated concepts: the fear of an English lingua-franca, the hope that multilingualism will promote better educational facilities for those who have traditionally lacked such facilities and a cultural appreciation for all the citizens of Europe.[124]

In *The Magazine: Education and Culture in Europe*, Issue 22, the first rationale presented in favor of the LINGUA program was entitled, "The limits of a lingua franca."[125] This magazine suggested that culture and language are inseparable and that the "lingua franca (English) does not equip the speaker to deal with all *country*-specific situations."[126] The article continued with an example of one of the major limitations of English dominance. "An Italian can be recruited in Germany for a job that requires mastery of English alone. However he will have to know German if he hopes both to become an integral part of the company, in which his fellow German workers communicate in German, and to feel at ease in everyday German society."[127] The main thrust of the argument presented is that "accepted diversity" of European culture must prevail over "forced unity." In other words, a Europe that is multilingual and accepting of

[122] Lingualia.net
[123] From the European Commission's Directorate-General for Education and Culture's periodical entitled, *The Magazine: Education and Culture in Europe*, Issue 22, 2004.
[124] Ibid.
[125] Ibid, page 4.
[126] Ibid, page 4
[127] Ibid, page 4.

its diversity is better equipped for the challenges of the twenty-first century than one that is English-speaking and culturally devoid.

As the European Union continues to politically and economically advance it has been argued that it must do so through the acceptance of all the cultures of Europe. Through the processes of unification, there seems to have emerged a sense of European *trans*-nationalism: a Europe that embraces its histories and diversity as a unifying force. It appears that European culture, based on minority languages and rights is valued because of their uniqueness to Europe. If the English language continues to dominate the cultures of Europe, then European culture is dead.

Although this language appears to be strong, these attitudes seem to account for the recently adopted linguistically oriented educational policies of the EU. The EBLUL and its interaction and promotion of Eurolang, Lingualia.net, and LINGUA, are all vital to the education of minority languages. However, in this era of globalization where information technology and economic policies affect and are affected by governmental policies, it is important to realize how European IT related businesses working in conjunction with international and regional governmental organizations have also encouraged minority language and cultural development.

European IT-Based Companies, EU Institutional Cooperation and the Revival of the Region

Beginning in January 2000, a consortium of organizations planned a twelve-month program to utilize existing information technology as a way of reviving the education of regional minorities in the British Isles. Project DART as it was known, followed the American corporate model that had created an infrastructure of information technology and a large network of users in areas that previously had been un-wired. Essentially, DART created a "multilingual web browser specifically tailored for use by minority languages (who are) not currently catered for by the mainstream commercial browsers."[128] "The project was also created to establish and test a European software localization model for minority languages applicable to other products and other minority languages in the future."[129] The importance and ultimate success of the technology was due to the level of shared interest by all participants as well as the recent legislation that concerned the treatment of regional minorities.

The European Bureau for Lesser Used Languages (headquartered in Brussels and Dublin) had initialized the consortium in 1999, when its organization was legally recognized in Ireland. Witnessing the successes achieved by American IT firms and the increased standard of living in Ireland, the EBLUL decided to utilize the existing technological infrastructure (the American technological model) and promote its agenda focused on the revival and therefore education of Celtic languages. Sabhal Mor Ostaig, the only Gaelic college in Scotland, and Fiontar Dublin City University, a bilingual (Gaelic and English) university in Ireland, joined the consortium and were committed to creating the content for the browser. The universities had determined that the browser had to have a cultural and an educational dimension to provide both the bilingual and

---

[128] From the Opera Press Release of 12/21/2000 entitled, "Opera Software in Breakthrough Localization Process. The article discusses Project DART and its interdisciplinary participants: the EBLUL, four European Universities, and Opera Software ASA, a computer software from Norway. Accessed online at: http://www.opera.com/pressreleases/en/2000/12/20001221.dml
[129] Ibid.

monolingual speaker with a unique experience. If the Gaelic language browser lacked either the *technological* content of an English browser, or was limited in its cultural content, it was believed that the only people likely to benefit from the initiative would be the small percentage of Gaelic-only speakers; namely those over 65 years of age, who arguably would not have had an interest in purchasing the software in the first place.

So the EBLUL contacted Opera Software ASA, a high tech language software producer (and advisor to the EBLUL), and advised them on the creation of a browser and a software package that presented the whole array of Gaelic culture. The product known as "Opera," was marketed as a way of enhancing the web experience for the people in Ireland, Scotland, and Wales who desired to "surf the web in their own languages."[130] Although it seemed likely that the presence of Gaelic (both Scot and Irish dialects) web sites would enhance the number of Gaelic speakers in the British Isles (and beyond), the EBLUL utilized the newly established educational programs of the European Commission to ensure better results.[131]

Mercator Education and SOCRATES, organizations dedicated to the enhancement of education across Europe, were commissioned by the European Commission and advised by the EBLUL to study the revival of minority culture.[132] The results have suggested that the Irish language has not demonstrated significant growth, in relation to the growth of the English language in the Gaeltacht region of Ireland.[133] Yet the results outside of Ireland appear to be significantly different. Although it is outside the scope of the present study, certain authors have suggested that the historical presence of the English language (in Ireland) has made reliance upon the English language greater and more acceptable there than in other parts of Europe. For example, Italy or France have traditionally relied upon their respective national languages, Italian or French, in building ideas related to nationalism and economic importance and are therefore more likely to oppose the presence of the English language than are the people of Ireland.

Reaction of National Governments

The reaction of the national governments has been diverse. Entrance into the EU has prompted certain governments to create cross-border protection for its nationals in other countries, while attempting to protect minorities within its own borders. Recently the Hungarian government has vowed to spend 1 billion Hungarian Forints (around 3.846 million euros) on the creation of Hungarian-language television programs in Romania,[134] the largest step ever taken by the Hungarian government to ensure better protection for "its people" across its borders. Similar measures have been taken by the governments of

---

[130] Ibid.

[131] Sloane and Johnstone's chapter in Hawisher's (ed) *Global Literacies and the World Wide Web*, suggests that language-oriented or directed websites are not enough to create a revival of minority culture. Education is paramount to success, and in fact when the education has been utilized in areas experiencing information technology, the revival has been greater. Pages 168-170.

[132] The following website provides link for all of the funding activities of the European Commission concerning language learning: http://europa.eu.int/comm/education/policies/lang/languages/index_en.html Mercator Education and the SOCRATES Program have been given funding and research incentives to enable Europeans to speak numerous languages, including minority languages.

[133] The region of Ireland, known as the Gaeltacht possesses the largest percentage of Gaelic Irish speakers.

[134] This comes from Eurolang, the news agency for the lesser used languages of Europe, written by Aron Ballo on February 19, 2004 in an article entitled, "Hungarian government to spend nearly 4 million euros setting up Transylvanian Hungarian TV in Romania, meanwhile language discrimination continues." Accessed on Eurolang.net on 2/26/04.

Spain and France in dealing with the Basques, the Slovene government in dealing with ethnic Slovenes in Italy and Austria, and the Portuguese government in dealing with the Galician government; groups that have traditionally been seen as problematic across the borders.[135]

The most pressing concern for these 'protected minorities' has always been the reaction of the national government to this type of cross-border protection. Traditionally, the governments of Europe have reacted unfavorably toward the protection of groups it deems as unworthy of protection. Examples abound of Romanian officials discriminating against ethnic Hungarians,[136] certain Austrian officials referring to the Slovenes in Carinthia, (the location of the entire Slovene minority in Austria) as sub-human, whose desire should be Austrian nationalism, and mastery of the German language and Austro-German culture,[137] and French and Spanish officials demanding cultural uniformity in the Basque country with attempts aimed at economic exclusion. These are not the most severe examples; they merely typify the sentiments once expressed by the governments of the European Union.

The following case studies will explore the relationship between the nation-state and the region. They will focus on the historical treatment of specific minorities and the recent protection granted to these minorities by the EU and the national governments in the presence of information technology. The findings will examine the relationship between the minority group and the nation-state as a result of EU pressure and the expanding availability of information technology. Fundamentally, I will be exploring the ways in which regional minorities have been able to revive their local cultures because of the protection granted to them by the EU and their own national governments in the presence of information technology, the overwhelming power of the English language, and non-governmental organizations.

---

[135] The ETA, the terrorist group associated with the Catalans of Spain and France have always incurred the wrath of national governments, yet recently, both sides examined the importance of ethnic diversity and the increased level of autonomy of the Catalan people. The Slovene minority, since the creation of an independent Slovenia in 1992 has seen an increase in protection and freedoms. These occurrences have in many ways resulted in the increasingly stable relations between the Galicians and the Portuguese government concerning their treatment.

[136] Ballo's article entitled, "Hungarian Government to spend nearly 4 million Euros setting up Transylvanian Hungarian TV in Romania," page 2.

[137] Although the hatred of Slovenes in Carinthia began in response to Austria's disdain for Tito's Yugoslavia, the creation of the Republic of Slovenia has brought to the forefront of the debate a renewed sense of xenophobia. Concept came from Tom Priestly's article, "The Position of the Slovenes in Austria: Recent Developments in Political and Other Attitudes," *Nationalities Papers*; March 199, Vol 27, Issue 1, pages 103-114.

Chapter Five: The Slovenes of Friuli Venezia-Giulia

In the northeast region of Italy, known as the autonomous region of Friuli Venezia-Giulia, exists the entire Italian Slovene minority. A combination of history, national development, and irredentism has rendered the Slovenes "foreigners" in a region that they have traditionally called home.[138] "The Adriatic boundary region and in particular, Trieste, were commonly portrayed as the confluence of three European races, German (Teuton), Italian (Latin), and Slovene (Slav), each of which had related characteristics... Germans and Italians were considered as cultural equals: bourgeois, modern, nationally evolved and essentially Western... Slavs were considered backward peasants, lacking national consciousness, and Eastern."[139] Although these beliefs had been established during the nineteenth century, two World Wars, a genocide, and a tense Cold War period, many Italians of the Venezia-Giulia still believe that " the Slovenes are inferior and not to be trusted."[140] In terms of political freedoms and societal views the Slovene minority of the Friuli Venezia-Giulia have never been granted the privileges that other minority groups had been entitled.

Recent events however have changed the position of the Slovenes in Venezia-Giulia. The advances in information technology, the impact of economic liberalization, and the increased market value of the English language in Venezia-Giulia have led the Italian government to reconsider its policies on the Slovene minority. In addition to these non-governmental features is the high degree of political pressure in terms of minority protection. The creation of Slovenia in 1991, its entrance into the EU in May 2004, and recent language policies of the government in Rome have given the Italian Slovene minority an unprecedented strength and possible revival. The purpose of the following case study is to provide a background on the historical treatment of the Slovene minority in Venezia-Giulia, in particular the regions of Trieste, Gorizia, and to a lesser degree Udine, and the ways in which the aforementioned features of globalization *in conjunction with recent minority friendly legislation* have given the Slovene minority greater cultural and linguistic freedom. It will begin with a brief examination of the region before the outbreak of World War I.

Pre-World War I

Italy is a unified nation-state whose "nation" has yet to unite. This contradictory definition is testament to the fact that Italian unification was achieved in response to the arrangement of the international community in 1861.[141] In many ways its unification was based upon the realization of Machiavelli's, *The Prince*.[142] The Italian *state* was created prior to the realization (or at least illusory realization) of the Italian *nation*. Its unification

---

[138] The area known historically as Karantania is the ancient political home of the Slovenes. It is a region that would eventually extend into central Austria (12th century). Then in the 13th and 14th centuries a large part of Slovene land became part of the Hapsburg feudal system, which it would ultimately remain until the end of World War I. These ideas came primarily from two sources: Rogel's, works, The Slovenes and Yugoslavism, (1977) and *The Breakup of Yugoslavia and Its Aftermath: Revised Edition*, (1997).

[139] Sluga, Glenda. *The Problem of Trieste and the Italo-Yugoslav Border: Difference, Identity, and Sovereignty in Twentieth Century Europe.* Page 2.

[140] Conversation with a resident of Trieste concerning the Slovene minority who had made it quite clear that the Slovenes were foreigners in "his Italy."

[141] 1861 was the year of partial unification since Rome was still under French rule until 1870.

[142] One of the main goals set forth by Machiavelli was a unified Italy; one that could withstand constant invasion and/or threats by greater powers.

based upon culture and language had prompted certain governments and intellectuals to resort to strict policies of irredentism and fascism.

Because language unity has often led to the creation and expansion of cultural unity and economic inclusion, the standard Italian language, just like the standard French or German variety was enforced as a means of building national unity amongst a people who had *never* been historically united.[143] The historical presence of the Latin language, the mother of the Romance languages had created a sense of unity amongst the intelligentsia, but feudalism and diverse geography perpetuated a regionalism in Italy unlike most places in Europe. Latin had served the people of its empire, but after the collapse of the Roman imperial infrastructure, the Latin language had begun to transform into various linguistic, regional forms. "In Italy, it is believed that by the tenth century, the regional languages were sufficiently distinct from Latin and from each other to be identified by their specific names."[144] People from different regions spoke different languages. The people from Piedmont, spoke Piedmontese; the people from Friuli, spoke Friulian; etc.

Yet economic and/or cultural growth provided certain languages with larger networks of speakers. The Florentine language, spoken across the region of Tuscany seemed to possess a greater value than other languages because of its large number of speakers. Florentine therefore became the chosen language upon which unity was to be based. Vizmuller has suggested, "that around the fourteenth century, after the economic and cultural leadership of Tuscany and especially Florence was well established, a literary, written language, common to speakers of different dialects/languages became a cultural goal."[145] Economic goals were bound to cultural goals and Gellner's notion of a "high culture" resulted in the first attempt at a "standard" Italian language, based upon the "wealth" or perceived importance of the Florentine language.

To suggest, however, that an intellectual movement begun in the fourteenth century based on the promotion of Florentine resulted in a united Italy in 1861 (with the exception of the Papal States) would be a gross misrepresentation. In fact, in 1861, "the year of Italian political unification, it was estimated that only 2.5% of Italians (those living within the recognized borders of Italy) knew Florentine and that the remaining populations were still using their own languages."[146] For the people of Friuli and Venezia-Giulia (still separate until 1946), a people who had traditionally based their economic lives on agriculture, their own languages provided them with more economic and cultural practicality. It was not until the late nineteenth and early twentieth centuries that standard Italian (Florentine) was imposed throughout the region.

In the nineteenth century the Hapsburg Empire controlled the region known as the Adriatic Littoral (the provinces of Gorizia, Gradisca, Trieste, and Istria). The diversity of the region created an inconsistent labeling of territory with nationality. "Italian nationalists referred to the Hapsburg Littoral as the natural extension of the Italian-speaking Venetian region and named it Venezia-Giulia, in honor of an imperial Roman

---

[143] Keating's *State and Regional Nationalism: Territorial Politics and the European State*, Hemel Hempstead: Harvester Wheatsheaf, 1988.
[144] Ibid. Keating described Italy's unification process as one continually based upon the government's unwillingness to accept its diversity.
[145] Vizmuller-Zocco, "The languages of Italian-Canadiens," *Italica*, Vol.72, No.4, Winter 1995, page 512.
[146] Ibid, page 512.

past." [147] Slovene nationalists on the other hand, called the Littoral, Julijska Krajina (Julian March), in which they included the Slovene-speaking areas that had been incorporated within the Italian borders in 1866." [148] For the Slovene nationalists, the aforementioned provinces conflicted with modern national boundaries, for the Italian nationalists, territorial distinction defined ownership. [149]

This conflict, which could be seen as a result of Italian unification (1861-1866), had changed the perception of Slovenes in the eyes of many Italian intellectuals. Throughout most of the eighteenth and nineteenth centuries, the description of the "Slav" had been based upon economic criteria and a certain degree of sympathy or pity. The Slovene, or more generally, the "Slav" was seen as a peasant farmer who had a limited means of opportunity. But as Sluga has suggested, this classification changed in the era of Italian nationalism and unification. When at one time "Johannes Herder's description of the Slavs as an 'oppressed docile farming people,' had dominated public attitudes, only a few decades later, Francis Gibbon's depiction of the Slavs 'as being savages' and 'racially inferior to (Westerners)' had become the standard. [150] Many Italian intellectuals believed that the future of the Italian state rested upon Italian unity, a unity that was determined by all those within the borders of the recognized sovereign state.

The growing sense of distaste for those perceived as foreigners, resulted in the formation of the intellectually driven annexation policy known as "Terra Irredenta." At the end of the nineteenth century, the Adriatic Littoral was still under the control of the Hapsburg Empire, and was perceived by many Italian intellectuals as land that had been lost throughout history. Italian intellectuals perceived the multiplicity of nationalities in the Hapsburg Empire as an unnatural arrangement of territory and identity. Marinelli for example suggested that the Slavic inhabitants of the region were passive in the face of what he referred to as 'superior Italians.' [151] Italian culture for Marinelli was not only *subjectively* superior, but also *universally acceptably* superior to Slavic culture; a description that made an annexation of the region justifiable. If Italian culture were truly superior, then logically, the Slovenes would not resist Italian rule because even they (Slovenes) would value Italian culture as something superior to their own.

At the turn of the twentieth century, it had become apparent that the 1867 Austro-Hungarian constitution, a document heralded for its position on national equality, was losing credibility. The tide of nationalism had begun to overwhelm the apparent multi-cultural situation in the empire, and nationality questions began to heavily influence the government of Austria. "Gerard Stourzh argued that in the final decades of the empire's existence, 'the question of Austrian citizens *belonging* to a certain nationality, and the problem of finding when in doubt, to which nationality a person belonged' loomed large." [152] The Empire had begun to categorize its different national groups and a

---

[147] Sluga, page 13.

[148] Ibid.

[149] It must be added that a Slovene minority has existed in the modern district of Carinthia in Austria. The entire region that at one time had been under the control of the Habsburgs was divided following World War I.

[150] Ibid, page 15.

[151] Marinelli, *Slavi, Tedeschi, Italiani nel Cosidetto (Litorale) Austriaco (Istria, Trieste, Gorizia)* Venezia: Antonelli, 1885. Chapter One.

[152] Sluga, page 18. Also, Stourzh, "Ethnic Attribution in Late Imperial Austria: Good Intentions, Evil Consequences," in Robertson and Timms, *The Hapsburg Legacy*, pp. 70-75.

consensus had emerged that favored certain groups over others. For instance, Macartney suggested that Germans, Poles, and Italians were valued as culturally advanced; Germans, Jews, and Italians were economically advanced; and Kann had recounted that after Germans, Italians had reached "a most favorable status" of any nationality in the Empire; testimony to the fact that Italians were granted linguistic privileges in the school system.[153] This "status" gave the impression that the "Italian" was *cultured* and the "Slovene" was *uncultured*. In many ways it also portrayed the Hapsburg Empire as a complex governmental arrangement whose competitive national orientations were pitted in a struggle with one another as a result of the heightened nationalist tendencies of the surrounding nation-states.

During the first decades of the twentieth century, Italian nationalists (in Italy) had begun to strengthen their claims to the Littoral region. Through the promotion and creation of certain national/cultural organizations primarily located in Florence, Italian nationalists attempted to inspire those living within Trieste and Gorizia to accept Italian nationalism and label all other groups as inferior. One such enterprise was the widely read children's periodical, *Il Giornalino della Domenica*, first published in 1906.

Luigi Bertelli, the publisher of *Il Giornalino*, "aimed at cementing a sense of national identity (amongst the youth)… by providing a forum that assigned large space to letters, contributions, and news from Trieste and by recruiting many young Triestines into the ranks of its ideal 'Repubblica dei Ragazzi' (The Republic of Children), an alternative form of government designed to put into practice the (Italian) nationalist ideology."[154] First published in Florence in 1906, *Il Giornalino* made a deliberate effort to nationalize the regions in the Empire that Bertelli deemed as *culturally* Italian. For instance, "postal letters from Trieste were never included under the rubric 'Lettere dall'estero' (Letters from Abroad), as one would normally expect, given Trieste was under Austrian rule."[155] The letters were presented as those written by Italians from a place (Trieste) that was within the sphere of Italian culture.

In 1910, Italian nationalism, based firmly in the tenets of *terra irredenta*, had perpetuated the creation of the "National League," an organization dedicated to the promotion of Italian culture in all parts considered "Italian." Since Trieste was considered under the sphere of Italian influence, the National League funded afternoon school programs throughout the city. However, one of the largest after-school programs was centered in the St. James quarter of Trieste. "This was significant because St. James, was (and to a large extent still is) populated mainly with Slavs, particularly working-class Slovenes… who made up between 20 and 25% of Trieste's overall population according to the census in 1910."[156] Because Italian and Austrian nationalists deemed Slovene culture inferior, it was seen both as a threat to the policy of *terra irredenta* and a source of instability to the Austro-Hungarian government.

---

[153] Sluga, page 18. Macartney, *National States and National Minorities*, page 142. Also, Kann, *The Multinational Empire: Nationalism and National Reform in the Hapsburg Monarchy 1848-1914, Vols. 1 and 2*, page 265.
[154] Pizzi, Katia. "Birth of a nation: The national question in Vamba's *Giornalino della Domenica* (1906-1911). Vamba referred to the pseudonym of the founder Luigi Bertelli. Page 1.
[155] Ibid, page 2.
[156] Ibid, page 4.

World War I and the Rise of Italian Fascism

Although racial discrimination had been present prior to the outbreak of World War One in the Littoral region, it was worsened by theories concerning race, the change of national boundaries, the labeling of Slovenes as socialists, and the collapse of the Hapsburg Empire. The cities of Gorica and Trieste exemplified this sentiment. Cities under the control of the Austro-Hungarian kingdom for centuries, Gorica, (renamed Gorizia after the First World War) and Trieste were placed under the control of the Italian government and within the newly established borders.[157] During the interwar period Gorizia and Trieste served as border cities between Italy and the newly created Kingdom of the Serbs, Croats, and Slovenes.

Beginning with Salvemini's "Questione dell'Adriatico," (1916) and furthered by Seton-Watson's journal, *The New Europe* (1916-1919), the question of the borderlands appeared to have been solved by a combination of irredentism and international involvement at the expense of the Slovene and Friulian minorities.[158] A new "logic" had entered the international discourse. Salvemini, who at one time had been considered a traitor by his Italian nationalist contemporaries, eventually argued that Italy must be given the rights to Venezia-Giulia because of Italian cultural superiority. In the "Adriatic Question," Salvemini "described the Littoral as a place of ill-defined nationalities and 'ethnic zones.'" [159] Salvemini stated that, "In Venezia-Giulia, 'the two nationalities mixed with each other almost everywhere'"; "Gorizia exemplified 'the political indivisibility of the two ethnic zones"; and "in the ethnically mixed Eastern Adriatic neither of the two cohabitant nations could advance claims for an exclusive national right, however the 'Italian experience of the region made the Italians of Venezia-Giulia, ' 'the most cultivated and most refined social element' in 'mixed areas,' and gave Italy the right to rule over Slavs."[160]

The notion of "racial determination" was furthered by Robert Seton-Watson, the editor of *The New Europe*, who had determined that past government failure was in part due to the model of governance chosen by the Hapsburgs. At one time Seton-Watson had been a great admirer of the democratic principles set forth in the Austro-Hungarian kingdom, but by the end of World War I, his notions of what was considered *proper* governance had changed. Seton-Watson based his new logic on the theory that there existed a *racial-boundary* correspondence; a radical British and American theory that had emerged during World War I.[161] Seton-Watson stated that the new theory proved that it "lay in the general interest—indeed in the very logic of things" that the Hapsburg and the Ottoman Empires make way for a new European (and world) order 'determined upon mainly a racial basis,' 'that is, according to the principle of nationality.'[162] For Seton-Watson, the question that concerned the borderlands of the Adriatic was solvable, if one could demarcate boundaries around different national groups and orientations and "leave

---

[157] The document known as the "Secret Treaty of London," promised Italy the northeast territory once under Austrian control in return for Italian troops.

[158] The Friulians are a distinct minority that dwells in the Friuli Venezia-Giulia with the Slovenes.

[159] Salvemini's, *Questione dell'Adriatico*, (1918) pages 48-49; and Sluga's, *The Problem of Trieste and the Italo-Yugoslav Border*, page 28.

[160] Sluga, page 28.

[161] Sluga, page 29.

[162] Sluga, page 29. Seton-Watson, "Preface," *Europe in the Melting Pot*, London: Macmillan, 1919, page ix.

as few minorities as possible on the wrong side of the final line and to strike an average between ethnography and geography."[163] In relation to the Adriatic Question, Seton-Watson's ideas caused more problems than solutions considering that census data showed that Slovenes tended to live in the suburbs and the Italians in the cities; making a *clear* demarcation impossible.[164]

Nevertheless, wartime speculation was rendered useless by the actions of the Italian military. By the end of the First World War, the Italian army had taken advantage of a weakened Austro-Hungarian army and claimed the Littoral for Italy. Because the Italian government had made a "secret treaty" with the British government, the cities of Trieste and Gorizia were repositioned as Italian cities. This boundary was held in tact until the beginning of World War II, and a subsequent occupation and division.

The interwar period witnessed the emergence of Italian fascism, the conclusion of a process based on the irredentism and heightened nationalism of the nineteenth century. The Nitti government of 1919 realized that the expanded Italian border meant a higher degree of responsibility to both to the international community and to the "non-Italians" of the Friuli Venezia-Giulia. The responsibility of the government of Rome was to ensure freedom to all of the people in Italy regardless of their ethnicity, in return for their allegiance to the Italian government. Unfortunately, the way in which this freedom was enforced was not directly determined by Rome, but by the authority of the regional governments created at the end of World War I.

The future of Gorizia and Trieste was entrusted to the will of the civil commissioners of the region. Dennison Rusinow, has suggested that the level of treatment of the Slovenes varied from region to region.[165] For example, "in the province of Gorizia, north of Trieste, Slovene organizations were left relatively unscathed... yet in Trieste...the treatment was not as good."[166] The Triestine civil commissioner, Antonio Mosconi had the habit of labeling the Slovenes as not only "aliens" but also socialists, who could possibly spread their will across Italy and destroy the Italian government unless strong nationalist policies were enforced.

Inevitably, Mosconi "prohibited the use of the Slovene language in government institution and law courts...encouraged and offered ideological protection to burgeoning (fascist) extremist groups whose main targets was Slavs...and eventually burned down the 'Hotel Balkan,' the Trieste headquarters of Slovene cultural associations."[167] Although the Nitti and eventual liberal Giolitti government in Rome condemned the acts, the 1921 formation of the Italian Communist Party, composed mainly of the Serbs, Slovenes, and Croats in Trieste, forced the liberal party of Trieste into an ideological compromise with the Fascist party.[168] This created a formal dichotomy between Italians (now representative of both the Fascist and Liberal parties) and Slavs (representative of the communist party) that would forever label the Slovenes in Venezia-Giulia as enemies of the Italian government and Western progress in general.

---

[163] Seton-Watson, page 311-312.
[164] Sluga, page 32.
[165] Rusinow's, *Italy's Austrian Heritage 1919-1946*. Oxford University Press, 1966, page 97.
[166] Sluga, page 42.
[167] Sluga, page 43.
[168] Ibid, page 43.

Between 1922 and 1938, Fascist ideology created a sense of urgency throughout the Venezia-Giulia. The Italian government regarded its obvious diversity (strong German, Albanian, and Slavic segments) as an impediment to international success. It was understood that Italy was not and had never been part of the "Great Powers" association that had been responsible for the well-respected balance of power system that defined the nineteenth century. Interwar Italy (and most of the victors of World War I) had valued "race" as the basis for international power and stability, which validated the spread of *italianita* (Italian national identity and culture) in a destructive and vengeful manner.

Between 1924 and 1938…policies were enforced that transformed five hundred Slovene and Croatian primary schools into Italian language schools, deported one-thousand "Slavic teachers" to other parts of Italy, closed around five hundred Slavic societies and a slightly smaller number of libraries", changed Slav surnames into "'more aesthetically pleasing'" Italian versions, searched houses for Slavic literature, erased non-Italian graveyard stones, and created a *Tribunale Speciale per la Difesa dello Stato* that sentenced 106 Slavs to 1,124 years in prison and was responsible for countless executions." [169] Although the final years of Mussolini's Fascist Italy had focused upon the deportation of Italian Jews, about 70,000 "able-bodied" Slavs had been contained in concentration camps to stifle any attempted insurrection.[170] Fascism rested on the notion of a united Italy, based upon the belief that national identity was tangible, logical, and necessary to the stability of a powerful nation-state. It also unfortunately rested upon the notion that cultural superiority produced legitimate guidelines and territorial boundaries.

Friuli Venezia-Giulia During the Cold War

To understand the situation of the Slovenes of Venezia-Giulia during the Cold War one should examine it in two distinct periods; first, the period from 1945-1954, the time of Allied and Yugoslav occupation; and second, the period from 1954-1991 which culminated in the disintegration of the Soviet Union and the emergence of the Republic of Slovenia. Because ideological differences concerning the modes of production and military zones of occupation defined the Cold War narrative, it is important to realize that the situation in the Venezia-Giulia following World War II is in many ways a microcosm of the overall "East versus West" situation. It properly defined the biases of East and West and provided a deeper understanding of the communist versus capitalist labels, which in many ways only masked biases based on racial discrimination and nationalism.

The initial retribution brought forth by the Liberation Front of Yugoslavia, resulting in the genocidal episode known as the *Forty Days*, perpetuated the creation of a "Free Territory" occupied by the Allied Military Government and the Yugoslav government in zones labeled A and B respectively.[171] The *Forty Days*, referred to by many Italians as "their genocide," occurred in the summer of 1945 at the hands of the pro-communist Liberation Council and the Yugoslav Fourth Army.[172] By the end of the summer, statistics have shown that "pro-Yugoslav forces had arrested a total of six

---

[169] Ibid page 43.

[170] Ibid, page 58.

[171] The Forty Days refers to the initial occupation of pro-Yugoslav forces that targeted ex-fascists members of Venezia-Giulia. Because Yugoslavia aimed at the creation of a communist state devoid of national identities, Italians became targeted across the Venezia-Giulia and Trieste.

[172] The Liberation Council had been formed from the Liberation Front which successfully marched into Venezia-Giulia before the end of World War II.

thousand prisoners (mainly Italian) in Trieste and Gorizia, of which 4150 were later released; that 1850 persons had been deported, and 1,150 had never returned."[173] Both ethnic groups had defined this episode differently: Slavs tended to regard the *Forty Days* as retribution for the acts committed during the fascist regime; Italians tended to regard it as a genocide that was aimed at the destruction of Italian and Western culture.

Prewar and wartime hostilities emerged in new ideological varieties in Venezia-Giulia. The zones of occupation that had divided the "Free Territory" were symbolic of the competition between communism and democratic liberalism. Both sides presented arguments that made their own ideology seem more tolerant toward ethnic minorities. In July of 1945, the Allied countries created the Council of Foreign Ministers, a group of four "experts" representative of each of the Allies, whose purpose was to resolve the border question along Italy and Yugoslavia.[174] The Soviet representative, Molotov argued "Yugoslavia—which had played so heroic a part in the war—should have not only the city of Trieste and the adjacent peninsula but also a large part of Venezia-Giulia."[175] His arguments were based on the notion that only communism could properly stifle national tensions.

The American-British contingency, however, feared that Soviet influence in the Mediterranean Region could be disastrous to the revitalization of the weakened European state system. Yet, American representative James Byrne realized that the ethnic strife and discrimination toward Slovenes would most likely continue if "some" of the disputed territory were not ceded to Yugoslavia. Byrne suggested, "that the city of Trieste should remain in Italy but its port be turned into a "free port" administered by its users."[176] Enflamed at the suggestions, both the governments of Italy and Yugoslavia were determined to maintain the territory that they at one time had commanded.

The result set forth on February 10, 1947, in the Paris Peace Treaty, was the creation of a United Nations commission placed directly in charge of the Free Territory. "The Free Territory government was to comprise a governor appointed by the UN Security Council, an executive council, and a popular assembly... and in order to establish the neutrality of the new government, the Free Territory was promised its own currency, official flag, and coat of arms."[177] However, Zone A and Zone B remained under the military control of the AMG and the government of Yugoslavia, and a governor was never agreed upon by the Security Council. Throughout the next several years suspicion and racial animosity led to the fleeing of "ethnic Italians" from cities under the control of Yugoslavia and "ethnic Slavs" from cities under the control of the Italian government.

As the Cold War continued to intensify, hostilities emerged in Trieste as local Italians engaged the Allied Military presence. "Italian political and intellectual figures such as Carlo Sforza and Benedetto Croce criticized the Free Territory for depriving Italy of her 'dignity and legitimate pride.'"[178] "In Pula, Maria Pasquinelli, described as a former Fascist, assassinated Brigadier General Robin de Winton, commander of the local

---

[173] Sluga, page 91.
[174] Novak, *Trieste 1941-1954*, page 242.
[175] Herbert Feis' book, *From Trust to Terror: The Onset of the Cold War, 1945-1950*, page 124.
[176] Ibid, page 124.
[177] Sluga, page 141.
[178] Ibid, page 144.

British garrison."[179] This mayhem provoked the Yugoslav government "to accuse the AMG of sabotaging the international state with the aim of creating 'such a situation of disorder in Trieste that a permanent military occupation would be necessary.'"[180] These accusations forced the AMG to assert that the Yugoslav government was in the process of creating a communist conspiracy to gain favor amongst the locals in the region, appearing as if they were the true bearers of a solution. As a result, the AMG began to make statements that equated the term "communist" with the term "Slav."

"In October 1947, Colonel Robertson, the AMG deputy civil affairs officer, recommended the programming of, 'constant and effective anti-communist propaganda by radio,' and interestingly, through the "discouragement of bilingualism," 'as this immediately brings in the national aspect.'"[181] Communist organizations became "Slav-communist organizations" and eventually the AMG declared the area under their total control. Military governorship was never the intent of the AMG, who still desired a "Free Territory" but the British-American commanders felt that it was necessary in order to prevent the possibility of a Slav-motivated communist takeover.

In March of 1948, the concept of a Free Zone had ended. The British-French-American contingent had proposed a "Tripartite Declaration" that proposed the concession of the Free Territory to Italy on the grounds that the Yugoslav government had invalidated their involvement in remedying the peace by "nationalizing" their zone, and constantly attempting to spread the will of anti-democratic notions of governance. Nevertheless this unilateral decision was never embraced by the government of Yugoslavia who continued to see the presence of the AMG in Zone A as a threat to their sovereignty.

However, as a rift emerged between the Soviet Union and Yugoslavia at the international level, there also existed one at the local level. "Some local communists formerly loyal to Yugoslavia were outraged by Tito's actions;" while others were in favor of an independent Yugoslavia free from the imperial whims of Josef Stalin.[182] Regardless of the whims of the people of Zones A and B, each occupied-area experienced different "national" aspirations. The AMG had to deal with the notion of the 'Slovenes' now living as a minority within an occupied territory that had become Italianized once again.

Irony would define the last few years of occupation. For example, the Italian language was considered the only legal language of Zone A, yet Fascism or any beliefs perceived as Fascist were been outlawed.[183] The Slovenes became valued as a "minority problem," partly because they had been victimized by Fascist elements, but also because their treatment was dependent upon how the international community valued Allied occupation. If Allied occupation promoted Slovene rights as those equal to the rights of Italians, then nationalist clashes would have necessarily continued. If on the other hand, the Slovene minority was discriminated against by nationalist Italians and not protected by the AMG, the communist government of Yugoslavia would have gained a diplomatic advantage; recognition of the supremacy of communism in its platform policy based on nationalist repression.

---

[179] Ibid, page 144.
[180] Ibid, page 145.
[181] Ibid, page 145.
[182] Sluga, page 147.
[183] Ibid, page 147.

As a result the two zones remained. The signing of the London Memorandum of 1954, stipulated that Italy and Yugoslavia recognize its respective territory and their respective national minorities. Zone A was given to the government of Italy and Zone B was given to the government of Yugoslavia. What is ironic is the level of importance given to the concept of nationalism by the Allies in these last few years. It must be remembered that immediately following World War II, both the communists and the democrats agreed that nationalism was a poor way to determine boundaries. Yet following a decade of revolt and occupation, an eventual boundary was drawn that corresponded with *national* boundaries. Italians in Zone A were forced to live with a 20% Slovene minority and Yugoslavs in Zone B were forced to live with a 10% Italian population, however the boundary itself was believed to be suitable because it corresponded to ethnic communities and census data.

In 1975, the Treaty of Osimo was signed between Italy and Yugoslavia, reinforcing the designation of Venezia-Giulia as part of Italy and Istria as part of Yugoslavia. This document, arguably one of the most controversial documents ever signed by the Italian government, was greeted with a tremendous amount of hostility and public resentment in the region.[184] A month before its passage, a petition of disapproval was started in Trieste that eventually gained 65,000 signatures.[185] The local Triestine paper, Il Piccolo played a tremendous role in achieving widespread disdain for the treaty and it continuously tried to bring attention to the problem of Italo-Yugoslav relations, the fact that Slovenes were "not trustworthy."[186]

The Treaty "recognized the long-standing partition of the region through a proposed 'transfrontier industrial zone (a free trade area),' which included a 'mixed' infrastructure, and the creation and implementation of indemnities and greater protection for national minorities in both Yugoslavia and Italy.[187] Although these were the expressed goals of the treaty, many Italians regarded it as an attempt to provide Slovenes with resources "that they did not deserve," and Yugoslavia with territory it should never have been given in the first place.[188] In addition to these grievances, certain neo-fascist elements had emerged in the early 1970's in response to the Italian government's findings in the Risiera trial. The Risiera trials, which had reexamined the genocidal policies of Italian fascists in the 1930s and 1940s, had not been sufficiently balanced (from the Italian/fascist perspective) by an investigation into the infamous "Forty Days," that left many Italians dead in the *foibe* at the hands of Tito's forces.

The public outcry that developed from both the Treaty of Osimo and the Risiera trial was intensified by the destruction of Slovene schools, homes, and cultural organizations.[189] Many Italians argued that the Risiera Trial dismissed the atrocities committed during the "Forty Days" genocide and allowed the Slovenes a level of innocence and guiltlessness that they should not have been afforded. The years 1975-1991 were categorized by a continuation of discrimination against the Slovene minority.

---

[184] The legislation had been "pushed" through the Italian Parliament by the Christian Democratic Party, who were in the majority at the time. Many members of the DC showed great disapproval at its passage and said that they could not "accept the state's treachery" in agreeing to the treaty with Yugoslavia.

[185] Giuricin, page 97.

[186] Ibid, page 97.

[187] Ballinger, page 93.

[188] Tonel, (ed.), *Dossier sul neofascismo a Trieste 1945-1983.*

[189] Tonel, (ed) page 36.

Although the Treaty of Osimo was supposed to protect and promote the use of Slovene in schools and in formal governmental affairs in Trieste and Gorizia, the autonomous government of Friuli Venezia-Giulia continually denied its usage. Public outrage at the presence of bilingual signs and Slovene cultural organizations made enforcement of Osimo quite difficult. It has only been recently that the Slovene minority in Italy has achieved an unprecedented level of support in Venezia-Giulia; yet the support has come from the European Union rather than the government in Rome.

Slovene minority protection and revival

Since the collapse of communism, the creation of Slovenia in 1991, Slovenia's accession into the European Union in 2004, and the increased presence of information technology and the English language, the Slovene minority in Venezia-Giulia has received an unprecedented level of support and protection for its language and culture. The protection that had been created in the London Memorandum in 1954 and reemphasized in the Treaty of Osimo in 1975 had typically caused more resentment than progress. The Italian constitution, which called for the creation of Friuli Venezia-Giulia as an autonomous region (1964) and protection of the Slovene language in Trieste and Gorizia (Article 6), had never been enforced by the regional administration because its presence had always resulted in violence and an unpleasant reminder that the nation-state of Italy lacked unity.[190]

However, with the dissolution of Yugoslavia and the creation of the Republic of Slovenia in 1991, the Slovene minority in Friuli Venezia-Giulia has begun to gain protection in unprecedented ways.[191] In terms of political representation, the Slovene minority has two cultural organizations, the Slovene Cultural and Economic Union (which is left-wing) and the Council of the Slovene Organizations (which is Christian-Democratic). Both institutions were established to promote the use and protection of the Slovene language throughout Italy. For example, these "umbrella" organizations that represent the interest of more than 50 cultural groups, have created a Slovene theater, a Slovene daily newspaper, *Primorski Dnevnik*, and a political party called the Slovene Community.[192]

In many ways it has been the cultural organizations in conjunction with the European Union that have inspired linguistic minority legislation in Italy. In 1999, the passage of Language Law 482, "recognized as the greatest achievement concerning minority linguistic legislation in Italian history," emphasized increased protection and enforcement of language protection. In many ways, recent legislation has been enforced because of the integral relationship between the European Union and the Italian government. "Since the European Union has such a strong position on the protection of minority rights and the border region of Venezia-Giulia has always been exemplary of

---

[190] The Treaty of Osimo was greatly rejected because many Italians felt that the "border region" (Istria) would one day re-unite with the rest of Italy; Osimo ended those sentiments.

[191] It must be remembered that both the London Memorandum and Treaty of Osimo dealt primarily with the treatment of Slovenes in areas where there was a large presence of Slovenes, namely, Trieste and Gorizia; the Slovenes in Udine lacked similar protection because their numbers were and are significantly lower.

[192] Pozun, *Central Europe Review*, article entitled, "Trieste's Burden of History." Volume3, No. 6, February 12, 2001.

problems associated with minority groups, the Slovenes have gained an unprecedented cultural and political victory."[193] In addition to Language Law 482/99, the passage of the Law on the Global Protection of the Slovene Minority in Italy (Law 4735) has extended the protection of the Slovene minority in Italy beyond the scope of census data. Traditionally, minority protection has been determined by the number of speakers within a given area, city, region, etc. For example the treatment of Slovenes in Trieste had always been of the highest level because Slovenes continue to make up about 20% of the population; whereas treatment of Slovenes in Gorizia had always been spotted, and the treatment of Slovenes in Udine, had traditionally been non-existent.[194]

With the passage of the "Global Law on the Protection of the Slovene Minority in Italy," the Slovene minority has reached a level of protection never before witnessed in Italy. "The law's major feature is that it extends protection over *all* Slovenes in Italy, including those in the Udine region who have never before been protected."[195] This recent interpretation has refuted the logic of the London Memorandum of 1954. The London Memorandum was designed to provide "speakers' rights,' in Trieste based on historic discrimination and population demographics. Even the Treaty of Osimo (1975), which solidified the boundary of the once "Free Territory," provided linguistic and cultural freedom based on ethnic configuration of particular areas. The "Global Law on the Protection of the Slovene Minority in Italy," is revolutionary because it grants protection to anyone who claims "Slovene minority status," regardless of census data or ethnic demographics.

To use the term "backlash" to describe the situation in Italy since the law's passage in 2001 is to seriously understate the response. Even before the passage of the controversial piece of legislation, the debate in the lower house of the Italian Parliament witnessed Conservative opposition naming "over 1500 points" of "poor" legislation.[196] "Among the most "valid" of charges was the "supposition that it would give Slovenes more rights than Friulians."[197] In a discussion with an aid to a member of the Italian parliament, I was informed, "the Slovene minority is seen and has been seen as the source of most problems in dealing with minority rights in Italy because their "lobby" (Yugoslavia) has been transformed from a communist dictatorship to the European Union; from a government that we despised, to an organization that controls us." Even as Italian and Friulian protestors took to the streets of Udine and Gorizia in the summer of 2001, and certain Slovene organizations and homes were rioted, the government of Slovenia had begun to present the problems of "its people in Italy," to the EU created European Bureau of Lesser Used Languages. Since the EBLUL's role is to conduct a thorough investigation of minority treatment in a particular area, it has been the EBLUL that continues to attach the label, "problematic," to the situation in Friuli Venezia-Giulia.[198]

---

[193] Ibid.

[194] This is based upon the number of Slovene schools in Trieste, Gorizia, and Udine. There have been about 10 to 15 active Slovene schools in Trieste; 5 to 7 Slovene schools in Gorizia, and zero schools in Udine.

[195] Pozun, *Central Europe Review*, from the section, "News from Slovenia," Vol. 3, No.7, February 19, 2001.

[196] Pozun, "Trieste's Burden of History," page 5.

[197] Ibid, page 5.

[198] A conversation with three members of the Italian parliament on September 8, 2002. They continually expressed concern that "outsiders" have begun to control their legislative wishes.

Nevertheless, on February 14, 2001 the Italian Senate (upper-house) finally passed the legislation. February 14th marked the end of five months of debate in the Senate, a time where representatives from all of Italy protested both sides of the arguments. [199] One week before its passage, "the only Slovene party in Italy, The Slovene Community Party, held a press conference in Trieste… to announce two proactive initiatives: the publication of a brochure entitled, "Asserting the Slovene Language in Dealings with Public Administration," and the EU backed and sponsored, Office for Human Rights, which "operates within the party itself."[200] The Slovene organizations had decided to create a European-wide plea for linguistic preservation during the Senate's final debate as a way to ensure passage.

Successful passage was accomplished and the budgetary allocation for the Slovene minority was initially 44 million Euros.[201] This however, further stimulated more animosity within the region. From 2001-2003 the Slovene minority has received 3.5 million Euros/year from the government in Friuli Venezia-Giulia.[202] The public funds have been used to not only protect Slovene speakers but to promote the media outlets, cultural organizations, and educational facilities. For instance, in Friuli Venezia-Giulia there are numerous radio programs produced exclusively in Slovene (12 hours a day) and over the past decade there has been an increase in the number of Slovene schools and students.[203] Certain Italian officials in Parliament continued to argue that the law has damaged the Italian 'nation' and the rights of other minority groups.

In fact the leaders of the Movimento Friuli, the political party representing the Friulian minority in the regional parliament, have demonstrated the most recent wave of grievances. Language Law 482, passed in 1999, which was purposely written to enhance all of the regional minorities of Italy, had allocated only 1 million Euro to the revival project per year. Since the number of regional minorities in Italy was recognized as 12, the Friulian minority has been able to receive roughly 85,000 euros per year.[204] Although Slovene activists have argued the "market value" of the Slovene language as being more significant than Friulian; Friulian speakers outnumber Slovene speakers in Venezia-Giulia, 15 to 1.[205]

Information Technology, The European Union, and the English Language

Budgetary allocation and political debate have only been responsible for a part of the revival process. A tremendous amount of support has come from the certain regionally focused trans-governmental organizations, the region's rise in information technology, several new free trade opportunities, and the international strength of the English language. The following section will examine the ways in which the European

---

[199] The lower house passed the legislation on July 12th, it did not even get to the Senate floor until September.
[200] Pozun, "Trieste's Burden of History," page 7.
[201] Pozun, "News from Slovenia," page 1.
[202] EBLUL account of Slovene minority of 2001, 2002, 2003.
[203] A Euromosaic account of the school year 1993-1994 suggested that there were only 63 kindergarten, primary and secondary schools in Friuli Venezia- Giulia. After speaking with an aid to the director of the EBLUL (January 11, 2004), who is also the editor of the Slovene newspaper in the region, suggested that there are more than 85 schools. Euromosaic of 1994-1995 found at the URL, http://www.uoc.edu/euromosaic/web/document/esolve/an/il/il.htm
[204] Coluzzi, page 29 of his article, "Regional and Minority Languages in Italy."
[205] Certain census data reflects that Friulian speakers range anywhere from 350,000 to 750,000.

Union's focus on regional identity, the recently increased level of computers in the region, the opening of free trade zones in the south, and the "feared" high market value attributed to the English language have perpetuated a growth in support for the Slovene minority in Italy.[206]

Since the approval of the Maastricht Treaty (1992) and the subsequent creation of the Committee of the Regions, the autonomous region of Friuli Venezia-Giulia has seen an incredible growth in political, economic, and technological opportunities. In addition to the European Research and Development Fund (ERDF) which has contributed 3-6 million Euros annually to the Friuli Venezia-Giulia; the INTERREG Community Initiative and the CORDIS Project (The Community Reasearch and Development Information Service) have recently allowed the region to expand its development and aid its minority groups (Friulians included) in achieving positive legislative protection. These different projects have all developed in response to regional pleas and regional acceptance.

The first organization to be examined is the INTERREG Community Initiative. INTERREG was specifically designed to handle border disputes and create economic stability and competition. [207] In particular, however, its focus has been the border dispute between Italy and Slovenia. The program emerged in 1997 when it was believed that the Republic of Slovenia would most likely gain accession into the European Union. "The total cost of the program, including national and private-sector funding, is approximately 31 million Euros."[208] The money (granted by the European Commission) given to the INTERREG Community Initiative is based around three major priorities:

1. Ensuring the proper development and protection of natural resources and the environment via the creation of natural parks, theme tourism and the promotion of local products.
2. Breaking down the existing barriers between communities living on either side of the border by encouraging the exchange of know-how, creating common practices in local development planning and mounting schemes that take advantage of the similarities between the areas concerned.
3. Supporting the small business sector through the encouragement of cooperation between firms, the provision of investment aid and support to innovative schemes in the private sector.[209]

In short, the INTERREG Community Initiative was funded to support the transition of the Republic of Slovenia into the European Union. It however, resulted in the tremendous economic and technological growth of the Friuli Venezia-Giulia.[210]

---

[206] Certain EU level regional programs also have provided benefits to the Friulian minority of the Friuli Venezia-Giulia.
[207] Committee of the Regions' website found at: http://ica.cordis.lu. Accessed on May 1, 2004.
[208] IBID.
[209] Based on the Commission's press release IP/97/753 of August 13, 1997.
[210] The Universities of Trieste and Udine have both become recognized as major European institutes and the city of Trieste in particular, has gained international reputation for its Science Park that has both stimulated tourism and technological growth.

The CORDIS Project, another recently funded enterprise of the EU has expanded the purpose of INTERREG by providing cross-border solutions to the local governments and businesses of Friuli Venezia-Giulia. In 2001, as a result of its economic and technological growth, Friuli Venezia-Giulia gained acceptance into the CORDIS 'regional gateway service.[211] The Friuli Venezia-Giulia has gained entrance into the CORDIS Project because it "houses one of the main multisectorial science parks in Europe (in Trieste) and two leading universities (Trieste and Udine).[212] In addition, the "region hosts innovative organizations which have been strongly involved in European research, participating in more than 450 EU funded projects, features that have allowed the region to gain international support and recognition. "[213] The CORDIS website has been a major contributor to the development of the Friuli Venezia-Giulia because it lists all of the regions currently participating in the project. This 'regional listing' has given certain regions the economic power of traditional nation-states; it also has given the different minority groups an incredible economic and political boost.

One of the most significant statistics of Internet usage has traditionally concerned the language of most websites. Since the creation of the Internet, most users have had to possess both relative economic wealth and some proficiency of the English language. A study in 1999 suggested that 90% of the Internet WebPages were written in English. At this time, the number of primary English speakers in possession of Internet availability was around 70%. By 2001 however the number of primary English-speaking users had dropped to under 50% of all of those "connected;" and by 2003, that number was down to 36%.[214] This drop is significant because it suggests that places that were once "unconnected" have very quickly gained connection; it does not however suggest that the English language has lost its prominence. These figures merely reflect a pattern that suggests new users do not use English as their first language; they must possess some proficiency however.

Much of this progress in Friuli Venezia-Giulia has been motivated by steps to enhance the level of connectivity in the region. Slovene activists have been successful in not only the creation of more primary and secondary schools, but also the "enhancement" of those schools. A conversation in October 2004 with a principal of a high school in Trieste stated, "Schools that had at one time lacked basic phone lines, now have Internet access." And that although, "the quality of access is still low in comparison to other places (in the region), many high school students from across the region, have begun to communicate with Slovenian university students in Llubljana."[215]

---

[211] The CORDIS Project and the Regional Gateway Service of CORDIS have aimed to stimulate technological innovation through economic support. All of the information concerning CORDIS has come from their website: http://ica.cordis.lu Accessed on May 1, 2004.
[212] Ibid.
[213] Ibid.
[214] *GlobalReach*, Global Internet Statistics of 2003. Found at the URL, http://www.glreach.com/globstats/ Accessed on March 12, 2004.
[215] He told me that the access still utilized phone lines, but the lines had been updated to better handle internet connectivity.

Internet communication, via email from Trieste to Llubljana is significant because it has eliminated the traditionally high-cost of phone conversation.[216] The price of Internet access for most Slovene schools in Italy is now paid for by the budget allocated by the different EU specialty agencies (listed above), the Italian government in Rome and in Friuli Venezia-Giulia, and the Republic of Slovenia. If Internet access continues to grow (which is expected), and the border between Italy and Slovenia continues to "erode" then it is very possible that a large segment of Slovene-speaking "college-bound" students will enroll in one of Slovenia's two major universities; a feat that several decades ago seemed unfathomable.[217]

Because Italy has only Italian-dominant universities, historically the Slovene minority has had limited options in terms of a higher education in its language. Only about 5% of the Slovene minority had ever gone to a university in Slovenia.[218] The remainder of college level students who desired an education in their mother tongue went to the *Liceo pedagogico con lingua d'insegnamento Slovena*, a Slovene language institute in Trieste. Both of these degrees however were primarily used for the acquisition of the skills needed to become teachers of Slovene in Italy. Recently this has begun to change.

After an examination of Internet capabilities in Trieste and Gorizia it is plausible to assert that language and culture *are* being enhanced. In addition to the growing number of websites dedicated to the "plight" of the Slovene minority in both Carinthia (Austria) and Venezia-Giulia, there are web sites that offer linguistic instructions and cultural traditions that would have otherwise been forgotten by history.[219] The largest site committed to the maintenance of Slovene culture via the Internet is "The Slovenian Language Technologies Society," accessible at http://nl.ijs.si/sdjt/sdjt-www-en.html#institutions. The SLTS is an organization that provides links and helpful information for anyone interested in the history, culture, language and future of the Slovene people. It provides sections that contain information on language resources and services such as tutorials and translation software, academia and industry, associations and societies, teaching opportunities and resources, and other portals to all things Slovene.[220] The website also provides links to the different EU cultural organizations in an attempt to portray linguistic and cultural preservation as a *European* priority rather than merely a *Slovene* one. Interestingly, the website and the links are provided for the user in two languages: Slovene and English.

---

[216] Williams, "Italy and the Internet," Found at Webword.com. Internet use in Italy (as in most of Europe) is very expensive because of the high cost of local phone calls. Even as Telecom Italia, the national phone company promised to reduce rates, the ensuing privatization of the firm resulted in a price increase.

[217] Since the creation of the Republic of Slovenia in 1991 and passage of its constitution in 1992, most Slovenes in Slovenia had been better educated than their Italian counterparts. Only about 5% of Slovenes in Italy ever attended Slovene universities in Slovenia, this however is beginning to change.

[218] Republic of Slovenia's Ministry of Education, Science, and Sport. Website found at: http://www.mszs.si/eng/ministry/publications/development/pogl_03.asp.

[219] Eurolang.net provided by the EBLUL has an archive section committed to the plight of all linguistic minorities. In addition there is Eurominority.org, and a host of websites produced directly by the European Union and its multilingual education campaign.

[220] The SLTS is considered a virtual organization located in Slovenia that caters to Slovene enthusiasts. What is of interest to this dissertation is the number of people Venezia-Giulia familiar with the website. Every Slovene high school student with whom I spoke, was very familiar with the website. The website is written in two languages, Slovene and English.

With the prioritization of the Slovene minority on both the agendas of the EU and the newly formed Republic of Slovenia, it is plausible to suggest that the Slovene population in Venezia-Giulia has emerged for the first time as a united entity. During much of the Cold War, the Slovene minority in Friuli Venezia-Giulia was a divided group. Known to Italians as either Reds or Whites, the Slovene minority had a difficult time addressing its own differences. The 'Reds', who had been described by Italians as 'traitors' for their affinity for the Yugoslav regime had typically denied or resisted the wishes of the 'Whites' who had desired autonomy within democratic Italy. Minnich has suggested that the traditional views of Slovenes were based upon local and/or national orientation. Those that favored the autonomous distinction had typically favored "cross-border" legislation with their "brethren" in Carinthia, Austria.[221] It is therefore plausible to suggest that the "Whites" also posed a threat to the objectives of the national government in Rome. Recently however, the collapse of communism, the creation of an independent, democratic, and liberal Slovenia, and the increase in information technology seems to have reduced these divisions among the Slovenes.

Protests that at one time had been greatly disjointed and usually in Trieste have recently become more unified. For instance, in the wake of the passage of certain federal laws (Language Law 482 (1999) and the Global Law on the Treatment of Slovenes, 2001) and regional laws (The Fundamental Law of Friuli Venezia-Giulia, 1997) that were intended to provide minority groups the opportunity to use their own language in public matters, court, government investigations, applications, etc; most official documents had continued to be produced and accepted only in standard Italian.[222] The most blatant example of the Italian government's subtle refusal to grant this legislation is concerned with the issuance of census forms. The ISTAT, the Italian Statistical Institute, has historically been the organization most responsible for the collection of census information. The ISTAT has traditionally created questionnaires in only the Italian language. With the passage of minority rights legislation the ISTAT was supposed to provide questionnaires in the language of the minority speaker upon request. This service however has never been enforced in the Slovene communities and incorrect information has resulted in poor treatment and assimilation.

Recently however, the Slovene minority has united in an unprecedented way. Beginning in October of 2001 a Slovene coalition that included the Slovene Party, the two 'umbrella' cultural organizations: the Council of Slovene Organizations and the Slovene Cultural and Economic Association, and mayors of "seven ethnically mixed Italian-Slovene municipalities across the region" had begun organized protests and legislative pleas.[223] Article 8 of the Global Protection Law for the Slovenes in Italy states

---

[221] Minnich, "The Individual as author of collective identities: reconsidering identity formations within a multilingual community," from the edited book, *Vecjezicnost na Evropskih Mejah- Primer Kanalske Doline*, from Slori, Italy, 1996/

[222] The Slovene minority continues to face discrimination at the hand of the Italian officials who "accidentally" ignore the legislation concerning minority rights. Article by Vida Valencic of <u>Eurolang</u>, entitled, "Slovene minority in Italy, protest against neglection of Slovene language in census questionnaires." Written on 10/23/01 from www.eurolang.net. Accessed here at: http://www.yeni.org/news/archives/00000025.htm Also in an interview with Alex Scencic, a Triestine businessman. Mr. Scencic informed me of the subtle discrimination on the part of the government in terms of collecting census information.

[223] Valencic, page 2.

that, "the Slovene language is *permissible* in public administration and all official documents." Therefore, articles written in the Slovene language possess official recognition in Friui Venezia-Giulia.

ISTAT representatives have claimed that a privacy issue is at stake because the issuance of a questionnaire in only the Slovene language would violate the privacy of single citizens and would place them at a disadvantage. The Slovene minority however has concluded otherwise. The leaders of the Slovene Party are convinced that "it is an excuse to discriminate against Slovenes; citing examples of South Tyrol and in the Aosta Valley, two predominant German regions, where the census questionnaires have always been written in the German language.[224]

The Slovene organizations continued protests throughout 2002-2003, and most recently have received widespread attention from the European Bureau for Lesser Used Languages. The EBLUL has a strong connection to the region and has asked the Regional Council of Friuli Venezia-Giulia to "renovate" the Fundamental Law of the Region (first approved in 1963 under the "special statute"). The strong connection has to do with the fact that the current president of the EBLUL is also the chief editor of the daily Slovene newspaper *Primorski Dnevnik*, and the regional Slovene Community representative.[225] This Europeanization of the region seems to have connected the minority, in this instance the Slovene minority, with not the majority (Italy), but the super-majority (the European Union) and other minority groups.

With the accession of Slovenia into the European Union on May 1, 2004, the Friuli Venezia-Giulia should also experience a large surge in economic development and trade through open border and open port agreements. Historically, one of the major impediments to economic development in the region was its southern, external border with Slovenia The northern border, shared with Austria has persistently acted as a "principal cross-border pass between two EU Schengen Agreement neighbors, Austria and Italy; which made flows of traffic and invariably commerce, free and unimpeded."[226] The southern border had continually been bothersome because it represented both the border of Italy and Slovenia and more significantly, the border between a EU member and a non-member. As Slovenia continues to gain monetary privileges and standardization, the southern, external border will become as open as the northern one; thus creating a sense that a "Europe of Regions" is a reality.

In addition to the opening of the southern border, the cooperation of two historically competitive seaports should also further economic growth. As the ports of "Koper (Slovenia) and Trieste (Italy) begin to specialize in their own areas of international commerce and merchandise" both ports should bring a sense of partnership never before witnessed to the region.[227] Enhanced trade should bring prosperity and

---

[224] Comments come from Andrej Berdon, Regional Secretary of the Slovene Party as cited in Valencic's article, "Slovene Minority in Italy Protest Against Neglection of Slovene Language in Census Questionnaires."

[225] Mauro, "Multilingual region Friuli Venezia-Giulia to include linguistic rights in legal revision," from *Organizzazione per la Minoranze Europee*, on April 26, 2004. Found at: http://www.eurominority.org/version/it/actualite-detail.asp

[226] From Armstrong's chapter entitled, "Culture, Continuity, and Identity in the Slovene-Italian Border Region," in Anderson's edited work entitled, *Culture and Cooperation in Europe's Borderlands (European Studies 19)*, page 166.

[227] Ibid, page 161.

greater mobility as well. It is therefore logical to deduce that the role of the English language will also grow.

As the Slovene minority continues to gain strength because of the EU and certain technological advances, in many ways it is making its pleas to Europe in the one language most Europeans (and people of the world) understand: English. Even a Slovene activist who refused to tell me her name stated, "It has become apparent that we need to speak not only our language of choice, but the language of the world, which is unfortunately English." It is believed that the English language will provide people with better economic opportunities and more accessibility to the world. Where the Italian language had once been considered necessary for most people in the region, it now seems that English has taken over the role.

For both the Slovenes and the Italians, the English language has become a necessity, but it appears that the Slovene minority is more tolerant of the English language than its majority-based Italian nationals. In a discussion with several Slovene high school students in Trieste and Gorizia, I discovered that they felt the English language was slowly replacing Italian as the 'most important language in the region,' because English has allowed them the privilege and opportunity to speak to other minority groups across the world. One said, "We have lived under cultural oppression for so long... if English is to replace Italian, but grant us our freedom and a better job, we will gladly take on this *light* burden."

This was not the reaction I received from several Italian businessmen in Gorizia. Paolo Cruciato and Giuseppe Tedeschi, two investment bankers who assured me that they in fact could speak on behalf of "most Italians in the region," suggested that Venezia-Giulia was becoming "less and less 'Italian' everyday." Cruciato stated that he was "raised to learn Italian, and only Italian," because he lived in Italy, but now, "the region had become 'Slovenized' by the 'liberal' ways of the 'New Europe.'" The Italian region of Friuli Venezia-Giulia had always been a region of many languages (Italian, Friulian, Slovene, German) but now the English language seemed to be replacing Italian as the major "second language" of the region for both Italian and Slovene primary speakers. Mr. Tedeschi stated that, his "greatest fear is that the Slovene students in Friuli Venezia-Giulia will abandon the Italian language, for English...just because it appears to be more economically viable." This sense of *fear* is most distressing because it represents a fear of losing nationalism and therefore power, which in central Europe has typically fueled disastrous outcomes. The interesting feature of this perspective is that economic viability is one of the most important features in the standardization of a language. It is the reason for the creation of Gellner's High Culture and the motivation behind most of the concepts related to nationalism.

Most people in Italy still speak Italian. However it is becoming increasingly apparent that most Italians are also beginning to learn the English language.[228] What is of great significance to this dissertation is the emphasis being placed on the linguistic and cultural traditions of Friuli Venezia-Giulia. There is a concerted effort to enhance the rights of minorities, in this case the Slovenes, but an indirect, inadvertent attempt to enhance knowledge of the English language. The Italians in the Slovene-populated regions of Trieste, Gorizia, and Udine had rarely learned any language other than

---

[228] According to *Nations of The World*, English has replaced French as the second commercial language, page 729.

Italian.[229] Their refusal to learn Slovene was a conscious, two-part decision. First, it responded to the nationalist belief of a united Italy. For many, knowledge of Slovene demonstrated acceptance of Slovene culture; a culture they have historically denied.

Second, Italian refusal was based on economics. For many Italians, the Slovene language did not provide substantial economic benefits. This is evidenced by the fact that so many Italians have learned English. The English language provides an economic benefit to the speaker. Interestingly enough, the Italian people to whom I had spoken suggested that the "Slovene language was 'destroying' *their* identity as a people" because it represented a *foreign* culture. The English language however, is spoken by a much larger-number, yet it is viewed as a *necessary evil* because it has gained the level of a lingua franca and its presence appears unavoidable.

It is this recognition that has led the European Union to create an unprecedented level of support for regional minorities and levy its influence over the nation-states of Europe. In many ways, the minority rights legislation, information technology, and minority-centered non-governmental organizations that have overwhelmed the nation-states of Europe have been created in response to the overwhelming presence of the English language. As Italy continues to empower parties like the Alleanze Nazionale, the Lega Nord (two post-fascist parties) and the controversial Forza Italia!, the party of prime minister, Silvio Berlusconi, it is evident that there exists a tension between the traditional "rules" of statecraft and the new "rules" of statecraft.[230] The confederation known as the European Union, acting in an era of enhanced economic and political liberalism, could be said to have an advanced influence on the activities concerning minorities in Italy. The point of this case study was not to prove that a relationship exists between globalization and the revival of minorities. It was to explore the possibility that a relationship exists.

---

[229] Armstrong on page 166 suggested that very few ethnic Italians in Trieste speak Slovene, whereas almost every ethnic Slovene speaks Italian.

[230] As of March 2002, most of the political parties in the Italian parliament had voted in favor of an amendment that would make Italian the "national language." This amendment would resemble the French constitution that claims that French is the language of the republic.

Chapter Six: The Forgotten residents of the Venezia-Giulia, the Friulians

"Our language has been with us for centuries
it is a link to our past and a reminder that
we are Friulian."
--Angelo Ricca, a Friulian from Udine, Italy.

A conversation with Angelo Ricca, a resident of the autonomous Italian region of Friuli Venezia-Giulia had suggested that he had never in his life assumed that his language which had been discouraged (and outlawed) during his youth would be given protection by the 'New Europe.' He had long given up on his father's desire of a Friulian revival, but now he and his friends and family are witnessing a revived interest in Friulian language and culture as a result of the impact of globalization. "I speak to you in English because I realize that we can communicate with one another; you an American and me a Friulian. Italian is still necessary for me and my family, but English has become more of a necessity to my grandchildren these days… in fact, it appears that English has allowed my language to flourish again."

This conversation and subsequent exploration of the national and regional ordinances concerning Furlan (the local, historical name for the region, language, and people) appear to reflect a people who have been more in the midst of a *European* economic and political system than an *Italian* economic and political system. The focus of the following case study will explore the relationship between globalization (heightened level of technological capabilities, inclusion within the European Union, and the presence of the English language) and the revival of Friulian culture. It will begin with a background of the language and the people and conclude with an exploration of its revival.

Friulianita: The people and language of Patrie dal Furlan

The Terra Irredenta movement in Italy that had caused a great many Slovenes within the Venezia-Giulia to face discrimination during the twentieth century also affected the Friulian population. In an interview with Pietro Gaetano, a 76 year old resident of Udine, he told me that his parents had been victimized for speaking Friulian, a language considered "by Italians as a language just as foreign as the language of the Slavs in the south."[231] His comments suggested that Friulians consider(ed) themselves and are considered, ethnically unique from Italians. In fact, a 1932 language classification placed the Friulian and Italian languages in mutually exclusive categories. Friulian was considered a part of the "Romanic or Rhaeto-Romanic language family, along with Rhatian and Ladinic… whereas Italian was one that had three variants: Italian proper, Gallo-Italian, and North Italian."[232] If Friulians are not Italians, and Friulians are not Slavs, nor Germans, nor Frenchmen, who are they?

Friulian culture and character, described by the term *friulianita*, has long been valued as the remnants of Celtic culture established in northeastern Italy during the days of the Roman Empire.[233] In fact, the Friulian language emerged from the "bastardized"

---

[231] Interview in Trieste on October 16, 2003.
[232] Roland Kent, "The sounds of Latin: A descriptive and historical phonology," *Language*, Vol.8, No. 3, pp. 11-216, page 30.
[233] Heady, *Hard People: Rivalry, Sympathy, and Social Structure in an Alpine Valley.* Overeas Publishing Association: The Netherlands, 1999. Page 219.

form of Latin used by the overwhelmingly high population of Celts in Latin Aquileia; a colony created by the Roman Empire in 181 B.C.E..[234] It has often been this Celtic distinction that has often inspired animosity towards and animosity from *standard* Italian culture.

At the turn of the twentieth century the language situation in the Friuli region had changed considerably. What at one time the Friulian language was the only language of the Friulian people, the rise of Italian nationalism led to a strict policy of language standardization and uniformity. Gaetano stated that school days were drastically different for him than for his parents. Although neither of his parents had "gone beyond the first few years of school," both spoke Friulian at home and in school." Gaetano said that *his* "generation was bilingual; not by choice but by consequences." The consequences to which Gaetano referred were the rise of Fascism and the outcomes of the Second World War, namely allied occupation and border realignment.

Fascism in the Region

The rise in Fascism was especially strong in the northeast region. "The government in Rome 'Italianized' all of the Friulian names of towns, rivers, and mountains... Udin became Udine, Rodean dal Bas became Rodeano Basso, etc."[235] A poem written in 1938 by Pier Paolo Pasolini, still known in the region as the "Great Pasolini" for his vast literary works written in Friulian and his political opposition to the Fascist regime, displayed the cultural destruction of the Fascist regime: "Fascists didn't tolerate dialects/ signs of the irrational unity of this Country where I was born/ inadmissible and imprudent relatives in the heart of the Nazis."[236] Pasolini's opposition was based upon his desire to create a revolutionary movement in which the Friulian people would gain a voice in the eventual government and make Friulian something that was heard in places other than churches. [237] These attempts however resulted in an inadvertent isolation of the churches and a weakening of the movement.[238]

In addition to the Fascist opposition, the Friulian people had become engaged in a battle of two dominant ethnic groups and competing ideologies. On the one hand was the Fascist Italian government that desired the elimination of the Slavic influence in Venezia-Giulia; and on the other hand were the Slovenes, a Slavic people who desired protection from an unwilling government in Rome. The Friulians were neither Slavs nor Italians, yet most in Italy considered them at the very least, Western, which distinguished them from the Slovene minority who had often been criticized for their eastern origins.

In the years immediately following World War II, Allied and Yugoslav occupation in Venezia-Giulia damaged the rights of *stateless* minorities, not only

---

[234] Euromosaic language profile of the Friulian language. Found at:
http://www.uoc.edu/euromosaic/web/document/friula/an/i1/i1/html#2 Accessed on August 3, 2003.
[235] Cosolo, "The State of Friulian Today and Tomorrow," from the URL found at:
http://www.geocities.com/Athens/Styx/9982/today.htm Cosolo is a child of Friulian parents committed to the enhancement of the language of his people.
[236] Temporale, "Pier Paolo Pasolini: His Life," an online biography found at:
http://www.pasolini.net/english_bigraphia01.htm.
[237] Ibid.
[238] The churches in the region had always spoken in the regional tongues as a way of keeping their power and influence in the local communities. Pasolini's creation of the "Little Academy of the Friulian Language" acted as a force committed to publishing Friulian texts and Friulian activism; it unfortunately divided its ranks amongst those who favored its presence in the churches and those who desired its expansion.

Friulians, but Sardinians as well.[239] The London Memorandum of 1954 stipulated protection for the minority groups in the newly recognized Friuli Venezia-Giulia, however, this protection was based on the treatment of Slovenes particularly in Trieste and Gorizia.[240] The London Memorandum of 1954 was based upon the border dispute between Italy and Yugoslavia. As schools and churches in the Italian zone of occupation continued their practice of *Italianization* in Friuli Venezia-Giulia, the Italian language began to gain recognition as the language of the *intellectual*. Minority languages, especially Friulian had become valued as the language of the *peasant farmer*. It was believed that intellectuals or those who desired to become intellectuals used standard Italian, while it was the uneducated, peasant farmers who used Friulian.

In many ways, this description had validity. For centuries Friulian culture was able to thrive because its identity was based upon two apparent contradictions: migration and provincialism. The people of Friuli (found overwhelmingly in Udine and Pordenone) were migrant workers. Holmes' study of Friulian culture has suggested that the Friulians "have been moving for centuries between farming and wage labour; locally and abroad; daily or seasonally."[241] Friulian identity, much like any cultural identity emerged from customs and traditions associated with the areas in which the Friulian people lived, worked, celebrated, and prayed. However, the identity of the Friulian people was based upon the homes in which they were raised, the places in which they worked, and the region to which they would seasonally return. Friulian culture has always been dependent upon movement; therefore so too were its cultural characteristics.

The prospect of a Friulian linguistic/cultural revival had always been based upon a presence in the Friuli region; primarily in Udine and Pordenone. However, postwar unification with the Venezia-Giulia not only gained the region special status as an autonomous region in 1963, but this pattern of migration had rendered the Friulian identity more European than Italian. One could therefore argue that the Friulians had never experienced the economic need, or High Culture that Gellner suggested had created strong national identities or a desire to learn a *national language* like other identities in Europe. The Friulian people had traditionally been a bilingual people whose knowledge of *foreign* languages was based upon agriculture, subsistence, and migration; features that allowed the local language to survive in the region.

Today it is estimated that about 500,000 people living within the region's provinces of Pordenone, Udine, and Gorizia speak Friulian.[242] There is also evidence that suggests that the language has never had as many 'unified' speakers as it currently does. Traditionally, the Friulian language, like most languages, had numerous dialects that corresponded to the different regions in which the Friulian people lived. Recently however, there have been major attempts to unify *weaker* Friulian dialects and produce a *standard* variety of the language. One major breakthrough, was the 1986 "commission

---

[239] In this context, *stateless* refers to the minority groups who lack nation-states that border the region. The German minority of South Tyrol had German protection an even the Slovene minority, revered the state of Yugoslavia for its higher treatment of Slavic people and national minorities.

[240] This referred to Article 3 and 6 of the Italian Constitution that had made provisions for the treatment of minority rights. The Italian government continually ignored the demands of the Slovene minority, but at the very least, they were protected "in writing."

[241] Quote found in Fillipucci's chapter entitled, "Anthropological Perspectives of Culture in Italy," page 58 of David Forgacs' edited book entitled, *Italian Cultural Studies: An Introduction.*

[242] ISTAT census data for the Friuli Venezia-Giulia for the year 2000.

chaired by the Catalan scholar Xavier Lamuela that officially recognized *central* Friulian as the *standard* and called for its introduction into many public places.[243]

When a language gains standardization, it also gains speakers and therefore more prominence. This recent standardization has strong implications for the revival because it seems to have coincided with the recent minority rights legislation of the European Union. Throughout the Cold War era, the Italian government in Rome attempted to grant linguistic rights to the minority languages of the numerous regions. Article 6 of the 1948 Italian Constitution states: "The Republic shall safeguard linguistic minorities by means of special provisions."[244] Yet this provision did not refer to the regional minority languages of Italy; it simply referred to the languages considered worthy of protection by the Constitutional Convention.[245] The regional minority languages of Friuli Venezia-Giulia, those typically defined by communities that lacked the presence of a bordering nation-state, had to wait until 1969 to receive legislation that outlined their position.

In the late 1960s, *Movimento Friuli*, a Friulian political party was formed at the University of Udine in response to the expansion of the region to include Venezia-Giulia and the growing tension concerning the treatment of Slovenes in Trieste and Gorizia. Through the provocation of *Movimento Friuli*, regional legislation was established as a way to ensure the protection of all linguistic minorities in the region.

Regional Law 11/1969 of Friuli Venezia-Giulia was passed as a validation of Articles 6 and 3 of the 1948 Constitution. Regional Law 11/1969 called for "Regional interventions for the *development* of cultural activities and *subsidies* for the conversation, the utilization and the *development* of the bibliographic, historical and artistic heritage for the *development* of higher education and for scientific research in the region Friuli Venezia-Giulia."[246] During the 1970's the government of the autonomous region of Friuli Venezia-Giulia continually ignored the Friulian language for two major reasons. First, the Friulian language was never specifically mentioned in Regional Law 11. The regional parliament had difficulty in its identification of regional minorities and its disdain for the Slovenes in the south prevented any 'minority rights' legislation. Second, Regional Law 11/1969 lacked the proper means of empowerment. The word, *development*, lacked direction and focus. Regional Law 11/1969 failed because those in power could argue that its application granted minority groups protection to revive their own cultures; not have the government develop or revive the culture(s) for them. The vague nature of Regional Law 11/1969 combined with the industrial expansion of the region throughout the 1960s, damaged the revitalization of the movement.

During the 1960s, the Friuli Venezia-Giulia experienced a growth in industry. "The industrial development of Friuli created a centripetal force that drew workers back

---

[243] Coluzzi, "Minority Language Planning: Two Case Studies, Cimbrian and Friulian," March 2003 paper presentation held at the University of Bristol.

[244] Article 6 of the 1948 Italian Constitution.

[245] Article 6 was only intended to protect the individuals in the South Tyrol (Germanophones); Gorizia and Trieste (Slovenophones); and the Aosta Valley (Franco-Provencalophone). I say *intended* because the situation of the Slovenes had never reached the level assumed it would reach in 1948.

[246] Regional Law 11 passed in 1969 in Friuli Venezia-Giulia

from distant cities to the new factories, shops, and businesses of the 'patria.'[247] This impacted Friulian culture because it was the first time Friulians did not have to face seasonal migration. They embraced factory life and in doing so enhanced the power of the Italian language. This economic growth and reconfigured lifestyle overwhelmed the aspirations of the *intelligentsia* at the University of Udine and the Movimento Friuli; the main proponents of the revival.

The late 1970s and mid 1980s in Friuli (primarily in and around Pordenone and Udine) witnessed the emergence of what could have been described as a great cultural contradiction. The economic growth that had caused a great destabilization of Friulian culture during the 1960s and 1970s had also perpetuated an expansion of the intellectual base. With the standardization of the Friulian language in 1986, the University of Udine began teaching classes about Friulian culture and in the Friulian language.[248] This led to a growth in the number of Friulian speakers with interest in its preservation. However this same group of people who now possessed a higher educational degree, found the Italian language more economically viable, thus disabling the initial dream of a Friulian revival.

Recently however there have been major attempts at linguistic revival. The greatest barrier that had traditionally faced a Friulian revival was its lack of "official" recognition. All of the regional legislation passed prior to 1996 had failed to acknowledge the Friulian language. The Italian Constitution recognized the "linguistic minority" but not the language and Regional Law 5/1996 provided the Friulian language with official recognition, but lacked federal mandate. It was not until the passage of Language Law 482/1999 that things started to change.[249] Language Law 482/1999 was a federal law that not only recognized the minority languages, but the minority speakers as identifiable groups. Language Law 482/1999, Article II stated that, "The Republic defends the language and the *culture* of Albanian, Catalan, German, Greek, Slovenian, Croation, French, Franco-Provencal, Friulian, Ladin, Occitano, and Sardinian." Legislation at the federal level has empowered all of the groups mentioned because each minority community has a legislative bond with every other minority community.

Identification as stated in Article II was a tremendous accomplishment for the minority groups and Article IV of Language Law 482/1999 provides even greater support. It stated:

1. Besides the use of Italian in nursery schools, the use of the minority language is allowed in the development of all educational activity.
2. The primary and secondary scholastic institutions must *assure* the learning of the minority language and deliberate the development of the modality of learning activities of language and cultural

---

[247] Holmes and Quataert, "An Approach to Modern Labor: Worker Peasantries in Historic Saxony and the Friuli Region over Three Centuries," *Comparative Studies in Sociology and History*, Vol.28, No. 2, April 1986, page 212.

[248] The course that is presently taught at the University of Udine that deals with Friulian culture is entitled, "Friulian Language and Literature."

[249] Regional Law 5/1996 specifically recognized the Friulian language as a regional minority language of the Friuli Venezia-Giulia, however its enforcement was never guaranteed. Italian Law 482/1999 was the most important piece of legislation ever passed concerning minority languages in Europe because it lists the 12 minority languages of Italy. It was *state* legislation which provides greater enforcement and great budgetary allocations.

traditions of local communities.

3. The same scholastic institutions must carry out enlargement
   of the formative offer in the favor of adults.

4. The initiatives foreseen in number 2 and 3 are realized by the same
   scholastic institution using human resources at disposal,
   financial equipment and resources available with conventions.

5. When there is pre-registration, parents have to communicate
   to the interested scholastic institution if they want to make use of
   the teaching of the minority language for their children.

Language Law 482/1999 is arguably one of the most significant pieces of minority legislation because it allows the minority speakers to determine their own level of usage. The Framework Convention for the Protection of National Minorities and the European Charter for the Regional and Minority Languages, both stressed *universal* themes and protections. Language Law 482/1999 was not entirely based upon the previous Italian legislation; it was also based upon European legislation. When the Treaty of Maastricht was signed in 1992, and the Committee of the Regions was established as a way of ensuring the rights and privileges of minority communities and regions, the Friulian community benefited more from established *European* principles than just Italian ones.

The region of Friuli Venezia-Guilia has also benefited from the region's recent technological growth. As the Slovene population has been able to expand its IT potential, so too have the Friulians. In fact, the entire region of Friuli Venezia-Giulia has been able to expand its technological capacities. The aforementioned CORDIS Project (Community Research and Development Information Service) and INTERREG Programs of the European Commission have helped all of the minority communities in Friuli Venezia-Giulia.

Currently, the northern Italian regions of Piedmont and Friuli Venezia-Giulia are the only regions in Italy that currently receive the CORDIS Project. So the region of Friuli Venezia-Giulia has received a tremendous boost from the European Regional Development Fund. Speaking on behalf of the ERDF, Pierre-Jerome Hennin stated that the European Commission is committed to the allotment of 3-6 million euros per year to develop and maintain five main objectives: "e-public services, e-cooperative businesses, e-welfare, e-health, and the creation of regional networks."[250] These services are focused on the regional and European levels. In many ways it appears that the "New Europe" is being based upon the enhancement of regional instead of national identity.

Another interesting dynamic of this particular revival is its high level of minority resentment. Although the Italian parliament has recently criticized Language Law 482/1999, most of the minority groups that gained recognition were in full support of it. What has begun to occur amongst the Friulian population appears to be a backlash against both the Italian government and the Slovene minority. Since the *passage* of legislation and the *implementation* of legislation are quite different, the minority groups in Friuli Venezia-Giulia have continually petitioned the government. For many Friulians,

---

[250] From an EU online article entitled, "Structural Funds: Commission contributes 3 Million Euros to a program of innovative actions in the region of Friuli Venezia-Giulia, 2002-2003" found at:
http://europa.eu.int/comm/regional_policy/innovation/pdf/programme/friulivenezia_en.pdf
Accessed on March 3, 2004.

the implementation process, which was given recognition on April 11, 2001 and "officially published in the Gazzeta Ufficiale della Reppublica Italiana" on Septemeber 14, 2001, was entirely for the benefit of the Slovene minority.[251] Silvana Schiavi-Fachin, lecturer at the Faculty of Modern Languages at the University of Udine, has suggested that the "Friulian language needs stronger cultural growth supported by all those who cover important roles at the regional level in politics, culture, and education."[252] This statement, given in January 2002, suggests that legislation needs a Friulian voice in the different levels of government. The Slovene minority has two large cultural associations and a very well funded political party, the Slovene Union that speaks on behalf of its people in the regional and federal levels of government. The Friulians have several cultural and academic associations (The Friends of Furlan and the Academy of Fiuli) and the Movimento Friuli political party, but lack the economic clout of the Slovene minority. Although the Slovenes still face discrimination in Friuli Venezia-Giulia, they appear to have more support because of the influence of Slovenia on the economy of the region.

Recent developments in the Friuli region seem to have emerged as a result of a backlash against governmental support for the Slovene minority. However, the leaders of the Movimento Friuli have moved their pleas away from Italy and more towards Europe. As Slovenia gained acceptance into the EU in May of 2004 and their minority rights continue to gain protection, the Movimento Friuli has begun to heighten its revival process, making claims to its people concerning the two dominant presences in the border region: the European Union and the Church.

In his revival attempt, Movimento Friuli Secretary De Agostini has begun to present Friulian culture as a "European" culture. "Secretary De Agostini has described the goal of the Friulian 'nation' as 'European,' but at the same time, independent of any state."[253] He has suggested that the "former EC had been valued as the supranational context in which the movement could achieve its autonomous aspirations; and now, with the rise of the European Union and the high level treatment awarded to minority groups, success is eminent."[254] His goal is to re-establish a Friulian culture similar to the Basque revival in Spain; which has resulted in elected members of the Basque Party gaining participation status at the European Parliament.

The leaders of the Movimento Friuli have hoped to revive Friulian culture through the creation of a European identity and a denial of Italian culture. As Holmes has suggested, "the Movimento Friuli has attempted to "embed ethnic autonomy within a European context—rendering the Italian nation-state largely irrelevant."[255] The goal is therefore to create a Friulian identity that is devoid of traditional Italian nationalism. It is an attempt to create a sense of nationalism (Friulian nationalism) out of internationalism. The intelligentsia, assume that globalization, the EU, and different transnational groups will help revive a sense of friulianita; one that has long been dormant. They claim that revival and support will continue to emerge from Europeanization of the region.

---

[251] From the U.S. English Foundation of Official Language Research found at: http://www.us-english.org/foundation/research/olp/viewResearch.asp on January 1, 2004.
[252] Ibid
[253] Holmes, *Integral Europe*, page 22.
[254] Ibid, page 22.
[255] Ibid, page 22.

Furthermore, efforts have been made to *Friulianize* the churches in the northern areas of Friuli Venezia-Giulia; an attempt that at one time had very limited positive results. Heady had suggested that in the past, "it had been difficult to persuade the congregations to accept the use of Friulian in church... most often saying that they did not want their children to grow up ignorant of the Italian language liturgy, because they wanted them to participate in church services outside the region."[256] Recently however, the Movimento Friuli has been successful in convincing priests to conduct services in the Friulian language and the results have been positive. Heady has suggested that the church has had a tremendous ability attracting the "traditional Friulian worker."[257] This is a classic example of the elites, in this case the clergy, forming a political base amongst a peasant population. Although to define the churchgoers as 'peasants' might blur the reality, Heady is clear to suggest that the congregations who have wholeheartedly embraced the revival have been those that are "by no means intellectual."[258]

Many Friulians are beginning to realize that their presence in the region is understood better within a European and universal context. De Agostini, the Secretary of the Movimento Friuli has stated that "We (Friulians) are Europeanistic... Borders are political, not cultural."[259] The Friulians, like many of the regional linguistic minorities of Europe have become entitled to a voice in the context of Europe. Although it would appear that a group considered a "minority" within the context of Europe would have a much smaller voice than it had within the context of the nation-state; it appears that there is at least evidence to suggest the opposite.

Filippucci has argued that the emergence of an integrated Europe has cultivated the "consumer culture of Northern Italy," and has allowed the Friulians to experience greater autonomy and position in Europe.[260] Because a great deal of the recent legislation is based upon minority rights and cultural preservation, the Friulian people have begun to revive certain past rituals as a way of retrieving the past. One such revitalized ritual is known as a cidulas ceremony—a Celtic ritual in which the pagan sun god, Beleno, is worshipped through the act of fire-throwing.[261] This ritual, believed to first been held at the Temple of Aquileia, the site of the earliest Friulians, has recently provoked an intense nationalism and Christianity, rarely seen in Friulian history.

At a cidulas ceremony held in "Ovaro in 1992, Friulian priests sponsored a special throwing of the cidulas at the Plef—the main church in the valley" in an attempt to unite all of the people in the valley and reconnect them with their past heritage.[262] When the youth of Ovaro joined in the celebration they dedicated their fire to the dismay of many Italians saying, "this is for Italy which has never brought us any good."[263] This obvious attack suggests that the Friulian culture has been revitalized and re-imagined as something different than Italian culture. In fact, Heady has suggested, Friulians have

---

[256] Heady, *Hard People: Rivalry, Sympathy, and Social Structure in an Alpine Valley*, 1999, pages 217-218.
[257] Ibid, page 218. Heady suggests that the people that have recently embraced Friulian culture have been the "non-inetellectuals."
[258] Ibid, page 218.
[259] Holmes, page 22.
[260] From the book, *Italian Cultural Studies: An Introduction*, by David Forgacs, Oxford University Press, 1996, page 58.
[261] Heady, 219.
[262] Ibid, 219.
[263] Ibid, 219.

begun to view themselves or re-imagine themselves as "Celts or Nordic people—those associated with efficient Germans, rather than lazy and corrupt Southern Italians."[264]

Much of the recent dialogue on the streets of Udine, suggests that there is a strong cultural divide. It is a good example of Rosenau's 'fragmegration' theory.[265] The people of the northern Friuli Venezia-Giulia, seem to feel more Friulian, than past generations and less connected to the nation-state of Italy. Although most Frulians speak Italian as their primary means of communication, they currently do so as a part of Europe rather than a part of Italy. As Language Law 482/1999 begins to gain region-wide recognition and the schools in the Friuli-Venezia Giulia begin to actively teach the Friulian language, and the courts begin to allow pleas, official statements, and civil service exams in the Friulian language, the Friulian culture will most likely have greater visibility than it has in the past century. As Mr. Ricca has suggested however, most of the children in Udine desire to speak English, because of its global capacity. The future of Friulian culture is brighter than it has been for some time, yet it possibly has been brightened by the presence of globalization and the unification of a continent committed to regional protection and universal human rights.

---

[264] Ibid, 219.
[265] Rosenau's theory of fragmegration is based upon his idea that globalization is fragmenting the world while at the same time forcing a tremendous amount of integration.

Chapter Seven: Rusysns, Rusnaks, Ruthenians, Ukrainians, or Lemkos

Geographic proximity and cultural similarities have resulted in the creation of nations, states, governments, religion, territory, and history has continually perpetuated an identity crisis for both the individual *within* the particular community and the individual *outside* the particular community. Take for example Huntington's brief discussion concerning the work of Donald Horowitz and the identity of the Ibo. "An Ibo may be… an Owerri Ibo or an Onitsha Ibo in what was the Eastern region of Nigeria. In Lagos, he is simply an Ibo. In London, he is a Nigerian. In New York, he is an African."[266] Regardless of the veracity behind the identity of the Ibo (or any ethnic group), these divergent identifiers have had a tremendous impact on the lives and representation of the individuals living in that particular region in Eastern Nigeria.

The same can be said for the people that live, had formerly lived, or continue to live in the shadows of the Carpathian Mountains. These people commonly referred to as Carpatho-Rusyns, Rusyns, Rusnaks or Transcarpathian Ruthenians have been identified as a nationality that has lived and continue to live in the "borderland" region known as the Subcarpathian Rus'. Alexander Musinkain has described the Ruthenians as "the eastern Slavic inhabitants of the northeastern part of the Carpathians. Geopolitically, the northeastern part of Slovakia, from the Tatras to southeastern Poland and sub-Carpathian Ukraine… the corner where Poland, Slovakia, and the Ukraine meet."[267] Certain Ruthenian national maps, investigated by Paul Robert Magocsi, have suggested that the Ruthenians have not only lived on the borders of these nation-states but in fact, have lived in certain Ruthenian pockets well within the borders of modern Slovakia and northeastern Romania.[268] Nevertheless, it has been their national identity that has served as the source of constant frustration amongst both the peasantry and the intelligentsia.

Because their "boundary" has existed within the framework of the modern nation-state system, distinct national and political influences have created a severe identity crisis amongst the Rusyns and amongst other national groups who have traditionally desired Rusyn assimilation into their respective national states. Ukrainian nationalists have argued that the Rusyns are Ukrainians, Polish nationalists have argued that the Rusyns, known as Lemkos in Poland are either Ukrainian or Ruthenian, and Rusyn nationalists have argued that the Rusyns are in fact, Rusyn; a distinct ethnic group that is neither Polish, nor Ukrainian, nor Russian, nor Slovak.[269] The basis upon which most ethnic

---

[266] Huntington's "Clash of Civilizations," *Foreign Affairs*, Agenda 1994, page 122.
[267] From an interview in, *The Slovak Spectator* by Andrea Chalupa entitled "The People from the Borderlands," of Volume 10, Number 5, February 9-15, 2004.
[268] From a map of Magocsi's copyrighted in 1993, found on page 6, of his edited work entitled, *The Persistence of Regional Cultures*, Columbia Press, 1993.
[269] Mysanyc, "From Subcarpathian Rusyns to Transcarpathian Ukrainians." Chapter One of Magocsi's edited book, *The Persistence of Regional Cultures*. Mysanyc is an example of the Ukrainian nationalist who has continually believed that the Carpatho-Rusyn/Ruthenian is in fact Ukrainian, due to geography and commonality of experience. Polish writers such as Olena Duc' –Fajfer, "The Lemkos in Poland," Chapter 3 of Magocsi's, *Persistence of Regional Cultures*, Roman Reinfuss, "Stan I problematyka badan nad kultura ludowa Lemkowszczyzny," *Etnografia Polska, 5* (Warsaw, Wroclaw, and Krakow, 1961) pp. 63-68; and Marian Jurkowski, "Lemkowszczyzna: materialy do bibliografii," *Slavia Orientalis, 5,* (Warsaw, 1962) pp. 525-536. The Ruthenian writer Paul Robert Magocsi in numerous works: *Carpatho-Rusyn Studies: An Annotated Bibliography, Volume I, 1975-1984*, (NY: 1988); *The Persistence of Regional Cultures*, (1993); *The Rusyns of Slovakia*, (1993); *The Shaping of National Identity: Subcarpathian Rus', 1848-1948* (1978);

claims are made, rests almost entirely upon geography and language.[270] Since the region known as the Subcarpathian Rus' (Transcarpathian Ukraine) has historically experienced both political and geographical shifts, the language and culture of the Ruthenians has shifted as well.

Magocsi has suggested that the "Carpatho-Rusyns are linguistically and culturally an East Slavic people who live along a linguistic-cultural boundary, the other side of which is inhabited by West Slavic (Poles and Slovaks), Finno-Ugric (Magyars), and Romance (Romanian) peoples."[271] Culture and ethnicity are difficult terms in the absence of national governments (or at the very least, political motivation), so the "real" borders of the Carpatho-Rusyns have been a continuous challenge for Rusyn scholars who have attempted to address the fundamental question, "To what degree are Carpatho-Rusyns distinguishable from fellow East Slavs, specifically the Ukrainians of neighboring historic Galicia?"[272]

This question rests upon claims presented by Rusyn nationalists that, a Rusyn culture exists or at the very least had existed at some time. Because Magocsi has presented the greatest amount of research on the existence and persistence of Rusyn identity and several governments have determined Rusyn culture as authentic, it will be assumed that a Ruysn identity does in fact exist or at the very least, that it exists to the degree that Basque, Occitan, Kurd, or any stateless national identity exists.[273] What must be examined, however, is not so much the *veracity* of the claims, but that Rusyn culture and language are so unique and persistent that a revival of it is even possible. This is the preface to the overall case study.

Thus, the purpose of this case study is twofold. First I will attempt to provide a historical background on the experience of the Rusyn people in Central and Eastern Europe. My initial focus will be their presence and treatment within several Central and Eastern European states prior to the collapse of communism. Secondly I will examine the more recent events that have impacted the revival of Rusynism; namely the impact of EU inclusion, the increased presence and scope of information technology, the increased level of economic inclusion, and the hesitation witnessed by the government of Ukraine.

Within this last section I will also be examining the claims presented by the foremost expert on Rusyn identity, Paul Robert Magocsi in terms of language use and national identity in the face of these phenomena. Magocsi has recently claimed that globalization, i.e. the growth in information technology and heightened economic mobility and European interconnectedness has allowed the Rusyn people to experience a

---

"The Ruthenian Decision to Unite with Czechoslovakia," *Slavic Review*, Volume 34, No. 2, (June, 1975) pp. 360-385, etc.
[270] Magocsi's claim has consistently attempted to prove that the Rusyn language is not merely a Ukrainian dialect as Mysanyc has suggested, but a language that has that possesses its own dialects based upon the place in which it is spoken.
[271] Magocsi's article entitled, "Mapping Stateless People: The East Slavs of the Carpathians," *Canadian Slavonic Papers*, Volume 39, Issue 3-4, page 304, 1999.
[272] Ibid, page 304. Galicia had been part of the old Austian-Hungarian kingdom, but it has been part of Poland since the conclusion of World War I.
[273] I make reference here to certain nations that have been widely accepted by the fact that certain territories coincide with the language and the culture of the particular nation.

revival based upon a reliance on the English language.[274] Because this dissertation has attempted to explore the relationship between globalization and minority linguistic and cultural revival based on the weakening of the nation-state and the strengthening of minority cultures and minority languages, I will continue this exploration with the Rusyns. The purpose of this case study is not to prove that the Rusyn identity has been elevated because of the English language, but to explore the possible relationship between information technology, the English language, and the increased power and influence of the European Union on the revival of the Carpatho-Rusyn culture in several nation-states.

I must begin this section, however, with a brief look at the person most responsible for the scholarship of the Carpatho-Rusyns, Paul Robert Magocsi, and his role in the revival.

Paul Robert Magocsi: The Scholar and National Awakener of the Carpatho-Rusyns

If one were to examine the literature of Eastern European national minorities written in the English language, one would come across the name Paul Robert Magocsi. Although Magocsi's contribution to the field of migration/national studies is primarily connected to the Carpatho-Rusyns, it is the most well researched, historically justified, body of work relating to any national group in Eastern Europe. Magocsi is not only the leading scholar in a field of academics committed to the theoretical underpinnings of national revival, he also is one of the major reasons for the revival that is currently underway in the several Eastern European countries that claim Rusyn heritage.[275] Magocsi is therefore more controversial than other theorists because it appears that he is responsible for the recent results that he has claimed have appeared on their own.

However Magocsi had not always been consumed with Rusyn culture. As an undergraduate at Rutgers University, he had been a student and activist of Ukrainian culture and politics. It was not until his years as a graduate student, and in particular his summer in Prague in 1968 that the focus of his research changed. "The Prague Spring had loosened the official Ukrainian grip on Rusyn cultural institutions and a distinct Rusyn identity began to emerge. The use of standard literary Ukrainian was no longer a prerequisite to get published, and parents began demanding the introduction of Rusyn into elementary schools to stem the tide of Slovakization."[276] Magocsi witnessed these events in person and began to both sympathize with the plight of the Rusyns and assess the implications and reality of a truly unique Rusyn identity. From that moment in 1968 to the present he has published over "550 studies in various disciplines—history, bibliography, language, cartography, political science—dealing with Central Europe and

---

[274] Concept refers to Chapter 38 of Magocsi's book, *Of the Making of Nationalities: There is No End*, Volume 2, entitled, "The End of the Nation-State: The Revolutions of 1989 and the Future of Europe." Pp. 306-320, 1999.

[275] Valentin Moroz has claimed that Magocsi is the sole reason for the Rusyn revival. He is quoted as saying, "In the very center of this (Rutsyn) revival stands one word: Magocsi." Ziac has written a piece entitled "Professors and Politics: The Role of Paul Robert Magocsi in the Modern Carpatho-Rusyn Revival."

[276] Martin Fedor Ziac's article entitled, "Professors and Politics: The Role of Paul Robert Magocsi in the Modern Carpatho-Rusyn Revival," in East European Quarterly, XXXV,2, June 2001, pp. 218.

Ukraine... yet *more than half* of these works focus specifically on the Carpatho-Rusyns."[277]

In addition to his scholarly work Magocsi had become "awakened" by his own Rusyn heritage. Magocsi claims to have had Rusyn maternal grandparents who had "always referred to their nationality as *Carpatho-Rusyn*," and in 1971 he married Maria Cuvanova, "a native of the Rusyn village of Vysna Jablonka in Slovakia."[278] Both his work and identity revolve around the preservation and enhancement of a culture that prior to his research was deemed dead. Since the following case study deals with the historical events and recent advancements of Rusyn culture, and Magocsi is the primary source for most of the historical information presented, this brief biographical sketch was necessary to convey to the reader an understanding of his possible role in the revival of a people from which he has gained such notoriety.

Background of the Rusyn People until 1919

Magocsi has made the assertion that the language of the Rusyns is best examined through an investigation of five distinct historical periods.[279] Magocsi's claim is that the language of the Subcarpathian Rus' was developed over time and its usage was divided between the intelligentsia and the peasantry by means of influence and accessibility.[280] "Sometimes the intelligentsia chose a local vernacular, other times they chose a more widely spoken language such as Church-Slavonic, Russian, Ukrainian, Slovak, and periodically, they chose an entirely foreign medium, such as Latin or Magyar." [281] Because the Rusyns had chronically lacked political autonomy, standardization of any one language was virtually impossible.

Another problem that had historically plagued the Rusyns was a linguistic divide between the intelligentsia and peasantry. The intelligentsia had considered only those languages "worthy of literary forms" as important. However, this had traditionally isolated the language of the peasant from that of the language of the intellectual. For example, Church Slavonic, considered by Rusyns as a "strong language" led to an increase in the language known by peasant and intellectual alike as Slaveno-Rusyn.[282] Yet it was Church Slavonic that appealed to the intellectuals because it was a fully, functional, literary language of the intelligentsia in Russia and Ukraine, and many valued it, including Dobrovsky, Fogarsij, and Luckaj as a language that had the power to unite all of the Slavic people.[283] This type of language superiority or preference created a pattern of linguistic division that continued through the twentieth century.

---

[277] Entry written by Bogdan Horbal in the *Encyclopedia of Rusyn History and Culture*, edited by Magocsi and Ivan Pop, pp 300.

[278] Ziac, pp. 217-218.

[279] The five periods are: 1.) 17th and early 18th centuries, 2.) 18th century to 1848, 3.) 1848-1918, 4.) 1919-1945, 5.) 1945- present. From page 1.

[280] Magocsi claims that Church Slavonic or Latin were used quite often as the literary language of the people, followed by Russian, Hungarian, and Ukrainian depending upon borders and warfare. Ibid, pages 3-30.

[281] Ibid, pp 1. The claim is that the intelligentsia had often chose the language of the people based upon availability and necessity.

[282] Ibid, pp. 5.

[283] Magocsi refers to Ivan Filevic's book, *Iz istorii Karpatskoj Rusi: Ocerki Galicko-russkoj ziznis 1772*, Warsaw, 1972, pp.96) Frantisek Tichy's, "Josef Dobrovosky a Podkarpatska Rus," in *Josef Dobrovsky sbornik stati*, (Prague, 1929), pp. 332-343. Alexander Rot's, "Josef Dobrovoskij o jazyke zakarpatskich ukraincev," *Naukovi Zapysky Uzhorods'koho derzavnoho universytetu, IX*, (Uzhorod, 1954), pp. 254-260.

Throughout the distinct periods presented by Magocsi is the problem of a language divide based along the lines of an intelligentsia committed to a preferred "literary" language (both Magyar and Russian for a period just prior to the turn of the twentieth century) and a peasantry devoted to the local vernacular. Unfortunately in the area of linguistic preservation and prominence, it has typically been the language deemed acceptable to the intelligentsia that has often been furthered. The case of Slaveno-Rusyn versus Church Slavonic and later Russian is no different. Pan-slavism, fundamentally driven by the intelligentsia in Subcarpathian Rus' achieved incredible heights during the middle to late nineteenth century. But as *pan-slavism* grew, the vernacular declined.[284] In addition, the Rusyn vernaculars were considered weak for two main reasons: the Rusyn vernaculars favored local identity, as opposed to Pan-Slavic identity, and the Rusyn vernaculars were *spoken* languages instead of *written* languages.

Magocsi has explained that the 1848-49 revolution had caused a brief period of national awakening as certain Rusyn nationalists living in Hungary, Slovakia, and Poland (Galicia) united to discuss national improvements based upon political unification.[285] "The Subcarpathian Ruthenians hoped, in cooperation with the Slovaks, to achieve autonomy in Hungary, or to join in a territorial union with the Ruthenians of Galicia."[286] However as fear of the revolution spread, the Hungarian government decided to grant autonomy to certain national minorities in the form of representative districts, which stalled the notion of transnational Rusyn political unity for a time.

If the creation of districts hindered the political unification of the "Rusyn nation," it in many ways stimulated the growth of cultural activities.[287] "In Presov a literary society was founded in 1850, and the following year Ruthenian was introduced as a language of instruction in the Uzhhorod gymnasium."[288] These events perpetuated a strong belief in Ruthenian national identity and the willingness of the intelligentsia to invigorate a sense of national unity. Until 1867, there was a growth in the speakers of the Ruthenian dialects, but the Ausgleich ended the brief renaissance.

"Despite legal guarantees for nationality rights, the Budapest government soon implemented a policy of forced Magyarization which led to a rapid decline in the number of Ruthenian schools and the national assimilation of many leaders who came to be known as Magyarones."[289] It is during this time that the creation of certain national orientations became popular to many of the Ruthenian peasants. In an attempt to consciously avoid "Magyarization," certain groups "found temporary refuge in the Russian culture... organizing several Russian-language publications."[290] Others attempting to copy their Ruthenian brethren in Galicia began to acknowledge the success of the Ukrainian language and made it part of Ruthenian identity.[291] At the end of the nineteenth century, the Ruthenian peasants, the masses, the ultimate determinant of nationalism's success, acknowledged the prevailing fact that other languages had become

[284] Magocsi, *The Language Question Among the Subcarpathian Rusyns*, page 8.
[285] Magocsi, "The Ruthenian Decision to Unite with Czechoslovakia," *Slavic Review*, Vol. 34, No.2, pp. 361.
[286] Ibid, 361.
[287] Ibid, 361-362.
[288] Ibid, 362.
[289] Ibid, 363.
[290] Ibid, 363.
[291] In Galicia, the Ukrainian language had been introduced in the form of textbooks in most of the schools.

more beneficial to their safety and economic involvement than the tongue of their Ruthenian ancestry.

1919-1945 in the Subcarpathian Rus'

Between 1919 and 1945, Magocsi has suggested that the language question, "reached its most controversial stage."[292] "After the breakup of the Hapsburg Empire, Subcarpathian Rusyns found themselves in the Spring of 1919 within the new state of Czechoslovakia, a democratic state where the Subcarpathian Rusyns were allowed to ferment."[293] Because the linguistic history of the Rusyns had been so intertwined with the perceptions and actions of the intelligentsia as well as the geographic proximity to certain states, three factions emerged amongst the Ruthenians: Russophiles, those with great affinity towards all things Russian; Ukrainophiles, those with great affinity towards all things Ukrainian; and finally, Rusynophiles, those with great affinity towards all things considered Rusyn.[294] Each variation attempted to weaken the identity of the 'other' as a means of strengthening its own faction. The Russophiles were fearful of any attempts at the spread of Ukrainian identity, the Ukrainohiles were fearful of any Russian influence, and the Rusynophiles were fearful of both persuasions because they valued both as foreign identities..

The Russian language and influence had traditionally played a major role in the identity of the Rusyn people. Beginning in the middle of the nineteenth century with the presence of Russian literature and the impressive power of the Russian army, the people of Transcarpathia had begun to value the perceived superiority of Russian culture.[295] As a result of this attitude, many Rusyns still in a confused state about their national identity "equated the local sense of 'Carpatho-Rusynism' with 'all Russianism.'"[296] Mysanyc has claimed that during the 1920s the Russophile intelligentsia in Czechoslovakia went beyond the level of influence and into the realm of indoctrination. Mysanyc's verbatim account of one particular Russophile program in 1926 is quoted here:

> "Can we call ourselves Rusyn?
> We can because Russian and Rusyn mean the same thing.
> What is our nationality?
> Russian, because we are the Russian people.
> And what is the size of this Russian people?
> There are over 100 million Russians combined.
> Who are the enemies of our nationhood?
> Our principal Enemy is the Communists, or the Bolsheviks.
> What is their attitude toward the Russian nationhood?

---

[292] Magocsi, *The Language Question Among the Subcarpathian Rusyns,* page 14.

[293] Ibid, page 14-18.

[294] Ibid, page 14-18.

[295] Magocsi quotes the supposed national awakener, Alexander Dukhnovych, and his statement concerning the brilliance of the Russian army in 1849. "One thing really gave me joy in life and that was in 1849 when I first saw the glorious Russian army... I can't describe the feeling of gladness at seeing the first Cossack on the streets of Presov. I danced and cried with delight... It was truly the first, perhaps the last joy of my life." From Magocsi, "The Ruthenian Decision to Unite with Czechoslovakia," *Slavic Review*, Vol. 34, No. 2, pp. 362. Originally from Dukhnovych, "Autobiography," cited in his *Tvory*, Published in Bratislava and Presov in 1967-1968), Volume 1, pp106-107.

[296] Mysanyc, "From Rusyns to Ukrainians in Transcarpathia," page 24.

They claim that for them all peoples are equal, but in actual fact they have sold the Russian people out to the Jews.
Who are the Ukrainians?
They are the next worst enemies of the Russian people after the Communists.
So then, our language is not Ukrainian?
No, there is no Ukrainian language, just as there is no Ukrainian state."

During the 1920s and 1930s it had become commonplace for the term Carpatho-Rusyn to mean Carpatho-Russian.[297] Russophiles amongst the Carpatho-Rusyns also ignored and refuted both the Ukrainophile and Rusynophile notions of national orientation because both were seen as contradictory to their platform. Russophilism and Ukrainophilism were created as a response to one another's notions as much as they were separate, individual, national identities.

Most Ukrainians, past and present, have argued that the Russophilism of the interwar period was perpetrated by Russian nationalists in an attempt to gain favor amongst a "weakly" defined Carpatho-Rusyn population, who were in fact, Ukrainian.[298] Writing in 1932, "one of the leaders of the Communist organization in Transcarpathia, Borkanjuk, exposed the social and class reasons behind the question, "why do they want to make us into Carpatho-*Russians*?"[299] The "us" referred to the Ukrainophiles. By 1937, Borkanjuk had suggested that the Russophiles had become adamant about the destruction of Ukrainian identity amongst the Carpatho Rusyns and had argued that the Russian influence had attempted to "detach the Transcarpathian Ukrainian population from its culture, because in this way it was easier to denationalize it."[300]

Since all Rusyns, regardless of their affinity were under the control of the government of Czechoslovakia, a democratic government that had never endorsed an *official* language policy, certain Ukrainian authors had suggested that the Rusyn population was allowed to foster a Carpatho-Rusyn identity, separate from both the notions of the Ukarainophiles and the Russophiles, in hopes that it would limit the power and influence of the state of Ukraine.[301] As a result, the Rusynophiles began to encourage support for the use of their mother tongue and their distinct national orientation. This revival was somewhat furthered after World War II and the placement of the Carpatho-Rusyns under the control of the Hungarian regime. The language, referred to as Uhro-Rusyn was codified in March of 1939 by the Rusyn grammarian, Ivan Harajada in his work, *Hrammatyka rus'koho jazyka*, which provided a language text aimed at the promotion and cognition of the Rusyn language.[302] Although the revival appeared as a

---

[297] Ibid, page 24.
[298] Ibid, page 24.
[299] Mysanyc, "From Rusyns to Ukrainians in Transcarpathia," page 25, of Magocsi's book, *The Persistence of Regional Cultures*. Mysanyc quotes, Borkanjuk from *Who are we and where do we belong?*, 1932,. Published Uzhorod, 1976.
[300] Borkanjuk, *Who are we and where do we belong?*, page 107.
[301] Mysanyc has argued this concept in his chapter, entitled "From Rusyns to Ukrainians in Transcarpathia." Magocsi discussed the work of Julijan Revaj, who in a book entitled *V borot'bi za pravdu: promova na Vseprosvitjans'komu zjizdi*, claimed that the Russian language was an "artificial" language for the Carpatho-Rusyn people often and properly referred to as Transcarpathian Ukrainian.
[302] From Magocsi, *The Language Question Among the Subcarpathian Rusyns*, page 23. Also, Harajada, *Hrammatyka rus'koho jazyka*, published in 1939, 1941 in Uzhorod.

positive step motivated by the Rusynophile intelligentsia, it was arguably safeguarded by the actions of the Hungarian regime.

In 1939, the Hungarian government outlawed the teaching and usage of the Ukrainian language, "grudgingly tolerated the claims of the Russophiles, and came out in full support of a distinct Subcarpathian Rusyn nationality and language."[303] As Magocsi has suggested, certain Hungarian officials had argued in favor of the Carpatho-Rusyn language and culture because it was considered a "weak" nationality compared to Ukrainian or Russian identity.[304] The Hungarian officials argued in favor of the Rusynophiles because Rusyn culture was valued as the "best way to assimilate eventually the (Rusyn) population into Hungarian culture."[305]

Unfortunately, the revival that had been experienced as a result of two Hungarian regimes (one immediately following the Treaty of Versailles in 1919, and the other granted in 1939) ended as a result of the expanded power of the Soviet Union at the conclusion of World War Two. Part of the area that had been controlled by the Hungarian Kingdom and the 20th century governments of Czechoslovakia and Hungary had become known as the Transcarpathian Oblast of the Ukrainian Soviet Socialist Republic, while another part remained in the northeastern part of Slovakia; the area known as the Presov region.[306]

Post World War II to the Collapse of the Soviet Union:
When Lemkos and Rusnaks became Ukrainians and Slovaks

Following Soviet occupation, the Ruthenians of the Transcarpathian Oblast and the Presov Region of Slovakia were forced to sever ties to their only identifiable characteristics: their language and their religion. Although a strongly defined written and spoken language had always been difficult to codify for the Ruthenians, the Greek Orthodox Church had traditionally served as the strongest feature of Ruthenian national identity. Magocsi has argued that the Greek Orthodox Church had functioned " both as a symbol and as a physical setting where interaction with one's own people took place."[307] The introduction of communism in Ukraine outlawed the Greek Orthodox Church and had created a school system that was dependent upon standard "Great Russian."[308]

The Soviet years were marked by an occupation and a denationalization of the Ruthenian people. When Poland and Czechoslovakia became part of the Soviet Union, successive communist governments labeled the Ruthenians, within their borders, as Ukrainians, which resulted in forced assimilation or mass deportation. In Poland where the Ruthenians had been historically identified as "Lemkos," the new label "Ukrainians" "made it easier for the Communist Polish Government to deport them on charges of treason. "The Communist Polish Government argued that, as "Ukrainians," the Lemkos were part of those Ukrainians who helped the anticommunist Ukrainian Insurgent Army

---

[303] Magocsi, *The Language Question Among the Subcarpathian Rusyns*, page 23.

[304] In this instance, "weak" refers to "weakly defined" based upon the fact that the Carpath0-Rusyns had no "big brother state" in the region. This concept also comes from Magocsi in, *The Language Question Among the Subcarpathian Rusyns*, page 23.

[305] Ibid, page 23. Also Magocsi, *The Shaping of a National Identity, Subcarpathian Rus', 1848-1948*. pp. 246-249.

[306] Ibid, page 23.

[307] Richard Renoff's comment on page 104 of Magocsi's edited work entitled, *Of the Making of Nationalities There is No End*, Volume 2.

[308] Magocsi, *The Language Question among the Subcarpathian Rusyns*, page 25.

(UPA) still held up in the Carpathians engaged in battle against the Polish and Soviet authorities after the end of World War II."[309] Lemko identity had become synonymous with Ukrainian identity in the Transcarpathia, therefore, the Lemkos of Poland became enemies of the state.

The deportation of Lemkos following the communist takeover resulted in a redistribution of Lemkos across Poland and a great amount of national confusion amongst the people. The Lemkos, who had historically identified themselves as a unique national identity, were "accused of helping the UPA bandits," which implicated them as aiding insurgent Ukrainians at the end of World War II. However most Lemkos "actively rejected a Ukrainian identity and in fact, gave no aid to the UPA."[310] The redistribution and ensuing sense of identity loss was best summed up by Magocsi: "From late April to July 1947...The Lemkos were put on transports and resettled in the 'Recovered Lands' of western and northern Poland, that is in lowland areas that were completely foreign to their mountainous ways... leaving behind their houses and churches and homeland... (which was) resettled by Poles brought in by the government from other parts of Poland or from among Poles who were repatriated from the Soviet Union."[311]

In neighboring Slovakia, the Rusyn population, who had commonly been referred to as "Rusnaks" by ethnic Slovaks, had also been subjected to a strong identification and policy of Ukrainization that ultimately resulted in the creation of a Slovakian identity. "Beginning in 1945 the new Rusyn political and cultural organizations were renamed as standard Ukrainian ones... and in 1952 the Communist Party of Slovakia banned the term Rusyn, and replaced it with the terms Russian and Ukrainian in schools."[312] The Slovaks had traditionally valued the Rusyns/Rusnaks, as Ukrainians, who spoke a western Ukrainian dialect, which led the communist government to endorse both the standard Ukrainian and Russian language in the school system.[313] However, Rusnak identification with the Ukrainians of the Carpathians was valued as a dangerous association as evidenced by the deportation of Lemkos in Poland. Magocsi has continually argued that the acceptance of Slovak identity, by the Rusyns since the early 1950s, had been in response to two observations: the resentment of Ukrainian identity and the negative attributes given to the Rusnaks as supporters of the UPA.[314] These features both revolved around the "true" identity of the Rusnaks. Slovakian and Ukrainian standardization policies adhered to the assumption of Rusnaks as being western Ukrainians, originally from the Transcarpathian Oblast. This assumption had forced the people who had

---

[309] Magocsi, "The Rusyn Question," page, 4. Found online at, http://litopys.narod.ru/rizne/magocie.htm Accessed on March 3, 2004. In this same article Magocsi discusses the fact that the Lemkos were distributed amongst the former German lands of western and northern Poland, page 4.
[310] Sysyn, "On Lemko Identity," Chapter 27 of the book entitled, *Of the Making of Nationalities, There is No End*, Volume 2, page 124.
[311] Ibid, page 124.
[312] Magocsi, "The Rusyn Question," page 9. Footnote number 9.
[313] Musynka, Chapter 2, *The Persistence of Regional Cultures*, entitled, "The Postwar Development of the Regional Culture of the Rusyn-Ukrainians of Czechoslovakia," page 53.
[314] Magocsi has continually argued that the peasant Rusnaks of Slovakia have rejected a Ukrainian identity because of their proximity of Slovak culture and disdain for the policies implemented by the governments "of the East." This also perpetuated a Slovakization of the Rusnaks of the Presov Region. Magocsi, "The Rusyn Question," page 4. Mykola Musynka who has argued that the Rusyn people are really Ukrainians that speak a western Ukrainian dialect refutes this sentiment. Musynka, Chapter 2 of *The Persistence of Regional Cultures*, page 53.

identified themselves as Rusnak, Lemko, or Carpatho-Rusyn to assimilate into another nationality for the purposes of protection.

Recent Developments in Carpatho-Rusyn identity: The impact of globalization on local revival

With the weakening and eventual collapse of communism in Eastern Europe and the expansion of liberal tendencies to areas once under the influence of the Soviet Union, Magocsi has argued that the descendants of the people of the Subcarpathian Rus', have utilized the processes and results of globalization to revive a dormant transnational Ruthenian identity. For Magocsi, "the Rusyn identity had never died in the Carpathian homeland... it was just waiting for its moment to be publicly re-born."[315] This "re-awakening" or "rebirth" has motivated Magocsi to reanalyze the situation of the Ruthenians and to openly argue their case as a distinctly, unique national minority. The question remains however, is globalization alone driving the Rusyn revival? Or is Magocsi, in his utilization of the means of globalization, driving the revival?

In many ways, the answer to both questions is "yes." Both globalization and Magocsi are responsible for the revival of local cultures. Magocsi could be considered the modern day answer to Alexander Dukhynovich, the father of the Rusyn people, but the triumph of Magocsi is bound to his follower's utilization of the Internet, the increased usage of the English language, the expansion of the European Union, and the destruction of the communist bloc. The purpose of this last section is to explore the possibility that globalization and non-traditional governance is causing a revival of the Rusyn identity, and in particular, a revival of the Rusyn language. I will examine the effects caused by the collapse of the communist bloc, the expansion of the European Union and its once "Western-only" non-governmental organizations, an increased usage of information technology, and the globalization of the English language.

EU Expansion and its implications for the Rusyns

For decades a distinction has existed between the many peoples of Europe. This traditional dichotomy has focused upon the separation of an East and West. Western values, centered upon notions of democracy, liberalism, diplomacy and most vividly, capitalism had always stood in contrast to the supposed values held by those of the East. Yet this distinction was based upon governmental, rather than societal classification. The Warsaw Pact, the zone that had delineated Soviet influence from Western democracy, formed the basis of this prevailing notion and reinforced this East/West divide.

In the years following the collapse of the Soviet Union, a new distinction has emerged upon the European continent. Yet this new distinction is not based upon two competing economic and political ideologies, but one based on membership. The European Union has attempted to unite a traditionally based, highly competitive, nationalistic people under a supranational government that places a strong emphasis on individual rights, self-determination, and regional development. In the creation (or modification) of such an organization, the governments and non-governmental organizations have created a system of governance that has reinvigorated an East/West distinction. The new dichotomy to which I refer is based upon membership.

Since the collapse of the Soviet Union, most of the governments of Eastern Europe have attempted to gain membership in the European Union. Though this may appear to be beneficial for the overall 'people' of Europe, it has the potential to cause an

---

[315] Magocsi's, "Carpatho-Rusyn Immigrants in America," *Persistence of Regional Cultures*, page 172.

enormous amount of pressure between member-states and nonmember-states in terms of policy formation concerning minority protection. Given that the Rusyns are scattered across several locations in Eastern Europe, their protection is ultimately determined by those states that have been given entrance or expected entrance into the European Union. If the government of Ukraine continues to refuse the claims of the Rusyns of Transcarpathia, they could possibly be challenged by other EU member-states in which Rusyns reside and exert pressure on the government of Ukraine.

Several years prior to the creation of the European Union at Maastricht, the European Commission had emerged as the leader of the incorporation and protection of Central and Eastern European Countries (CEECs). Through a policy created in the "Phare Program" (Pologne-Hongrie: Assistance a la Restructuration des Economies) and a new directive, focused on the issuance of "direct grants for assistance", the European Commission became locked into direct bilateral and contractual relationships with individual recipient countries and had to invent a philosophy to sustain the program."[316] One of the largest and earliest obstacles was member-state reaction and concern regarding economic instability.

Because the former communist countries were valued by member-states as dysfunctional and oppressed there existed a level of hesitation concerning economic assistance. Sedelmeier and Wallace have identified these "principal characteristics as a focus on the normalization of relations," and "the provision of technical assistance."[317] The European Commission determined that certain countries were more stable and therefore, more trustworthy than others in Eastern Europe. Upon completion of this determination, the second policy of economic assistance was initiated. "From early on this approach established an asymmetrical relationship, in which the European Commission set the conditionality for assistance and ultimately, accession."[318]

For purposes of this case study, it is important to note the passage of the "democratic initiatives" placed into the budget line of the then European Community, by the European Parliament in 1992. This stipulation, which extended the existing Phare Program to ensure a "political" dimension based upon "civil society" proved to be a deciding feature of CEEC accession. After signing the Lisbon Report (1992) which focused on EU enlargement, and "distinguished between the countries of the European Free Trade Association (EFTA) as immediately eligible for accession; the "Southern applicants"(Cyprus, Malta, and Turkey) and the CEECs; in June of 1993, at the Copenhagen European Council, it was decided that CEEC inclusion was a recognized "goal" of the European Union.[319] Association with EU members and the "opening up" of the market had been the position of the European Commission. After 1993, *inclusion* applications had been issued to those countries whose democratic and economic criteria were strong enough to be considered part of the European Union.

"The Madrid European Council in 1995 decided: to ask the Commission to prepare its opinion on the candidates 'as soon as possible' after the conclusion of the next conference, due to start in 1996; to ask the Commission to a prepare a composite paper

[316] Sedelmeir and Wallace, "Eastern Enlargement," Chapter 16 of *Policy Making in the European Union*, Fourth edition, NY: Oxford University Press, 2000, pp. 433.
[317] Ibid, 434.
[318] Ibid, 434.
[319] Michaleski and Wallace, 1992.

on enlargement, both to evaluate the effects of enlargement on the EU's policies, particularly agriculture and the structural policies, and to make proposals for the 'financial perspective' from 2000 for the EU budget; and to set an indicative date to open accession negotiations with the CEECs..."[320] Following extended negotiations between the European Commission and the Central and Eastern European Countries over terms of accession, the European Council endorsed the prospective membership of 10 CEECs, plus Cyprus and Malta, at a summit in Helsinki in 2000.[321] The countries included were the Czech Republic, Hungary, Slovenia, Poland, Slovakia, Romania, Bulgaria, and the three Baltic states of Estonia, Latvia, and Lithuania. Hungary, Poland, Slovakia, and Romania all possess members of the Rusyn nation, and are therefore required to "provide institutions guaranteeing democracy; the rule of law; human rights; and *respect for and protection of minorities*."[322] Although Chapter 4 of the current project analyzed the social pressure placed upon existing EU member states, the pressure placed on EU applicants and non-applicants is arguably greater.

Subcarpathian Rus' and the EU accepted Rusyn Diaspora

This mentality however has not been consistent with the recent treatment of Rusyns elsewhere. The following section will explore the struggle of the identity of Rusyns between EU applicants and the government of Ukraine in this era of globalization. In addition to this, it will focus on and reinforce the claims of Magocsi that information technology and the presence of a global lingua franca (English) have empowered a Rusyn revival across Europe. Where it differs from Magocsi's assertions is in the area of linguistic revival. Magocsi has claimed that the English language will serve as the unifying force of Rusyns, *I will explore the possibility that the English language has caused many nation-states to allow a Rusyn language revival, to maintain their sovereignty and gain access into an international system, and thus demonstrate that "politics still matters."*

Recent Rusyn Successes in Poland, Slovakia, and Hungary: The Power of Technology, the Diaspora, and the European Union

In the Lemko region of Poland, the collapse of the Soviet Union has witnessed the successful creation and protection of two cultural organizations: the Society of Lemkos (formed in 1989) and the Union of Lemkos (formed in 1990.). Though the organizations maintain different perspectives on Lemko identity, both have been instrumental in the promotion of scholarly research, seminars, publications, festivals, and the promotion of their native language.[323] Michael Sandowicz, the head of the Society of Lemkos (Warsaw) has argued that the codification of the Lemko language is of utmost importance to a Rusyn revival because it is the foundation of their national consciousness and the Polish government has made provisions that legally recognize their status as a minority.[324] With the expected entrance of Poland into the European Union in May of 2004, and the continued reach of the global economy, Sandowicz has stated that

---

[320] Council of the European Union, 1995; page 23. Also in Sedelmeier and Wallace, page 445.

[321] Hancock and Peters, Chapter 35 of *Politics in Europe*, 3rd Edition, NY: Chatham House Publishers, 2003, pp. 537.

[322] Ibid, 537.

[323] Laun, Karen M., "A Fractured Identity: The Lemko of Poland," *Central Europe Review*, 12/5/99. The Society of Lemkos is a pro-Ukrainian (Ukrainophile) group, whereas the Union of Lemkos tends to be pro-Rusyn or Ruysnophile.

[324] Walton, Nicholas. "Lemk people fight for survival," *BBC Online*, Thursday, August 8, 2002.

increased usage of computer technology and in particular, the internet, will allow the Lemkos of Poland to openly communicate with the "Lemko diaspora in the United States and Australia (wealthier nation-states) and contribute to the project of revitalization."[325]

The most remarkable technological feature in Poland is both its ranking in terms of computer ownership and overall computer quality. Poland ranks fortieth amongst countries with computer capability, twelfth amongst countries based on the newness of the computers, and fourteenth in terms of its overall computing power.[326] Although quality of computing is essential, the distribution of Poland's technology is also widespread. A recent study has concluded that 62% of the young people in Poland use the internet at least once a week, [327] which is of significance to this study because it demonstrates that the Polish youth use information technology more often than even their EU member counterparts.[328] This high level of information technology has given the Polish minorities, including the Lemkos access to a cross border experience while allowing the government of Poland the recognition it has needed to gain acceptance into the EU.

The government of Slovakia had been hesitant in granting linguistic rights to national minorities until it received approval from the EU concerning accession in 1999. In 1995, the government of Slovakia recognized the Rusyn language as the official literary language of the Rusyn people.[329] However, one year later, the Meciar government outlawed any privileges granted to minority groups and stated that Slovak was to be the only language spoken in Slovakia. It was not until July 11, 1999 that official recognition was granted to minority groups. This recognition came as a direct result of strong, negative criticism from EU officials.

This official recognition was significant for two interrelated reasons: first, it paved the way for further Rusyn cultural activities, and second, it gave official status to a people who had never been officially recognized by the Slovak government as a unique ethnicity. "In Medzilaborce, a poor city of roughly 7,000 near the Polish border, Rusyns are the overwhelming majority"— and as Reynolds has suggested, "its Rusyn, not Slovak being spoken in the home, on the streets, in the pubs and at the churches."[330] Although its

---

[325] Ibid.

[326] From the list provided by Douglas Huang based on his survey from *Magellan's Log* from http://www.texaschapbookpress.com/computerusagecomplete.htm. The data was collected on July 12, 2000.

[327] From *Poland Development Gateway*, accessed at: http://www.pldg.pl/p/en/nw/2762

[328] Ibid. The article addressed the fact that only 56% of the youth across the EU access the internet on a weekly basis.

[329] Reynolds, Matthew J. "Rusyn Patriots Questioning Purpose of Linguistic Revival," from *The Slovak Spectator*. Accessed at http://www.iccweb.org/rusynback.htm on March 2, 2004.

[332] Matvey, David. "Ruthenian Language Rights Takes One Big Step Forward, a half step back in Slovakia, while Slovakia takes a Big Step Forward,"*Rusyn News and Information Service*, accessed at: http://www.legacyrus.com/NewsReel/RusynNews/SlovakLanguageLawPasses.html

[333] Ibid

[334]The one area that the Rusyn minority seems to continually face is its small representation as a linguistic minority. To be considered a national minority in Slovakia, a group has to reach a certain percentage of the population, the Rusyns are barely at the government level.

[335] Pozun, "The Rusyns of Hungary: End of the Millennial Struggle," *Central Europe Review*, Vol. 3, number 16, May 7, 2001.

[336] Article 68 of the Hungarian Constitution.

practicality is often the subject of debate amongst the locals and officials, the very existence of the language as a means of communication suggests that the government honors its presence.[331]

The same sentiment can be used to describe the progress of Rusyns in Hungary. In 1991 the Organization of Rusyns was formed which motivated the creation of several cultural societies; namely the Andy Warhol Arts Association (1995), the Rusyn Research Institute (1996) and the Rusyn Museum in Muscony (1998).[332] These cultural organizations were given the opportunity to enhance their scope within Hungary because at the time the government of Hungary was in its application process for EU inclusion. In Muscony where the number of grade school children studying in Rusyn has grown every year since the 1995/1996 school year, the Rusyn language has also been given its own media resources.[333] "The community has two primary publications, *Ruszinszkij Zsivit/Rusyn Life* and *Orszagos Ruszin/The National Rusyn News Bulletin*; and two television channels that broadcast on Channels One and Two on Hungarian Television.[334]

Although cultural projects appear to be quite significant to any revival, it has been the political system in Hungary that has allowed the Rusyn minority to flourish. According to Bryan Pozun, "Hungary has instituted what may be the most liberal minority policies in Europe, covering almost all of its non-Magyar residents. International observers have hailed the unique experiment of "minority self-government" as a significant step toward minority rights."[335] According to article 68 of the Hungarian constitution, "minorities (have) the right to collective participation in public life, the right to use their own languages, the right to use their own languages in schools, and the right to establish local and national self-governments.[336]

For the Rusyn minority, the collapse of communism, the desire of EU membership, and the larger technological presence in the communities has created a system in which the idea of Rusyn identity has reemerged.

Problems for the Rusyn Revival: Magcosi's Benevolent Lingua Franca and the Denial of Ukraine

While successes seem unstoppable in the face of globalization and EU expansion the major problem that continues to face the Rusyn revival is the problem that faces all linguistic revivals, namely, its practicality in a world that is increasingly becoming standardized by the presence of the global lingua franca. Since economic and educational motivation have been valued as important features in the development of national identity and therefore the "market-value" of the national language, the Rusyn language has always had a problem gaining support for its usage. Now however, it seems that the English language is replacing the national language as the most desirable means of communication, which seems to place the local Rusyn tongue at odds with its national counterpart. Reynolds in an article in the *Slovak Spectator* asked a local resident of Medzilaborce about his interpretation of the Rusyn Revival. The man answered, "The Rusyn language has no meaning in the context of Slovakia moving towards

Europe...when I see Rusyns, we, of course, only speak Rusyn, but I don't really see what the point would be in my son learning how to read and write in Rusyn... I would really like him to study English."[337] This is both a worry and a hope for many Rusyns in Slovakia's Presov Region because it signals a distinct change for Eastern Europe and the European Union.

It is a worry because it signals another setback on the road to revival. But it also suggests hope because it offers insight into the expansive usage and interconnectedness of areas in Europe that had at one time been disconnected. Magocsi has suggested that European expansion to areas of Central and Eastern Europe will perpetuate greater border crossing activities and will create a Europe of regions rather than nation-states.[338] His overall belief (and most likely, desire) is best summed up in the last few lines of his article entitled, "The End of the Nation-State." Magocsi writes, "The era of the nation-state as the most effective social and economic unit is over. The future belongs to smaller regions functioning together as an economic unit. Europe can and should show the way toward this new reality through the actions of the European Union, which must eventually encompass the entire Continent. It is this kind of future that will assure the well-being of national minorities in east-central Europe and thereby reveal that the revolutionary year of 1989 was truly the beginning of a new era and not a return to the old." [339]

Although this article was written in 1992 and revised in 1994, a few of Magocsi's claims and desires have proven true, yet others seem to have been proven false. EU expansion has witnessed the recognition of national minorities and certain economic benefits; however, Magocsi had also claimed that Europeans overwhelmingly value the English language as a positive feature in the creation of an integrated Europe that is respectful of its minorities.[340] His argument is based on the following premise: "In the new Europe... if a Catalan decided to spend his or her life in Catalonia, only knowledge of the Catalan language would be necessary...if on the other hand, the Catalan decided to live somewhere else in his or her new country in Europe, his or her initial and perhaps dominant language in the workplace would be English."[341] This argument would be valid if in fact the "new Europe" was as tolerant toward English as Magocsi has claimed.

Recent evidence has shown that the countries of Western Europe, those currently holding membership in the EU have made a concerted effort as is evidenced by the previous chapter to create minority language programs and IT software to enhance the diversity of languages. Since it is the Western European countries that currently make up the legislation in the EU, it can be at least argued that there will be an eventual strengthening of minority languages in central and eastern European countries because organizations like the EBLUL and the Committee of the Regions begin to finance fledgling programs in Slovakia, Poland, the Czech Republic, etc.--- all countries in which Rusyns reside. Therefore, I am not in disagreement with Magocsi's argument, I am merely disagreeing with his premise. Whereas Magocsi argues that all of Europe will

---

[337] Reynolds, "Rusyn Patriots Questioning Purpose of Linguistic Revival."
[338] Magocsi, "The End of the Nation-State: The Revolutions of 1989 and the Future of Europe," Chapter 38 of the book entitled, *Of the Making of Nationalities, There is No End*, Volume II.
[339] Ibid, page 320.
[340] Ibid, page 317.
[341] Ibid, page 317.

continue to "willingly embrace" the English language, I am exploring the possibility that market forces and economic inclusion have perpetuated the average European to "hesitantly accept" the new lingua franca, and in many ways allow national minority groups to practice their traditions, beliefs, and languages. The section will begin with a brief examination of this "hesitant acceptance" of the English language as a Rusyn identifier, followed by an examination of Ukraine in terms of American IT market penetration, IT usage, and EU involvement.

English language: Unifier and Divider

In recent years, the rise in the number of Rusyn websites has allowed members of the diaspora from around the world to organize conferences and create awareness of their situation of the unpleasant treatment of Rusyns in Ukraine. Although most websites are concerned with historical accounts of the Rusyns, recent sites have been committed to the greater organization of conferences such as the World Council of Rusyns, the World Forum of Rusyn Youth, and several online newspapers.[342] What is of interest to this dissertation is the number of Rusyn websites in the English language. Ninety percent of the Rusyn websites online are written in English.[343] This evidence would suggest that most people interested in Rusyn, have some proficiency in English. It also suggests that in many ways, Magocsi would appear to be correct in his assumptions.

However, for Magocsi to be accurate, the Rusyns (those living in Slovakia, Poland, Hungary, Ukraine etc.) would have to be willing to learn English as a way to strengthen support for a Rusyn identity, because knowledge of English would allow a greater sense of support from the Rusyn diaspora in North America. Recent evidence however, seems to suggest the opposite. At the most recent meeting of the World Congress of Rusyns and the first annual meeting of the World Forum of Rusyn Youth held 4-8 June 2003, the Rusyns of North America attempted to reinforce the concept of internet usage based upon the English language amongst their European-Rusyn counterparts, but were greeted with suspicion.[344]

The North American Rusyns expressed their desire to create Rusyn unity through commonality of speech and heightened technology, namely the English language coupled with internet growth. Because most North American Rusyns have been exposed to the writings and ideas of Paul Robert Magocsi it is not surprising that this is their prevailing logic. However, as many of the Rusyn Youth of North America had discovered in Presov at the First Annual World Forum of Rusyn Youth, their notion of unity based on technology and knowledge of English was met with a tremendous amount of disapproval.[345] As Zelimir Koljesar, a 22 year old attendee from Ontario, Canada had discovered, "The internet appears (to us) to be the great solution to communicate and get things done... however, only the people from North America, Germany, and Vojvodina

---

[342] The number of online resources that pertain to Rusyn identity and history is quite vast. A great deal of information comes from http://www.tccweb.org/Rusynback.htm; certain sites maintained by Magocsi; and several in the form of online newsletters such as the *Outpost Dispatch*, from the Rusyns of North America.

[343] Typing in Rusyn or any of its different varieties will present the researcher with a vast amount of literature on the Rusyn people in the English language.

[344] *Outpost Dispatch: Newsletter of Rusyn Outpost North America*, August 23, 2003. Most of the works from Rusyns of North America could not understand that the people with whom they spoke, spoke English, but did not desire Rusyn revival based on the internet.

[345] Ibid.

supported the idea."[346] English laden technology seems to be understood by the European Rusyns as a North American endorsement of an English-based Rusyn identity, which (for many Rusyns) is an unacceptable condition for revival. This has been expressed as of "great concern" for several attendees of the Forum because the characteristics of the internet currently contradict with the essence of the Rusyn people. The historical desire of national recognition and improvement is obviously benefited by technological advancements, yet these advancements are laden with the English language and therefore provide a tremendous contradiction. As Magocsi has claimed, most Rusyns comprehend the English language; however most do not value it as the final step in revival. For the European Rusyn, knowledge of the English language is merely the key to acquiring the internet and Western ideas, which will lead to more software and websites written in the Rusyn language about Rusyn culture.

IT Developments and Cross-Border Action in Ukraine

The most troublesome feature facing the Rusyns of modern Transcarpathia is their continued lack of recognition as a national minority in Ukraine. This is exemplified in the 1991 refusal of the government of Ukraine to acknowledge the Transcarpathian referendum of autonomy. As the nationwide referendum to gain separation from the Soviet Union was being issued, the people of Transcarpathia were voting on the creation of their own autonomous region within Ukraine. Although 78% of the residents of Transcarpathia voted in favor of regional autonomy, the government in Kiev ignored the referendum, claiming that there was confusion amongst the voters in regards to the question on the ballot and the "fact" that the people of Transcarpathia were not a distinct ethnic group, worthy of regional political autonomy.[347]

Based upon the necessary EU criteria, Ukrainian involvement with or accession into the EU will not be possible in the near future. However recent developments within the Transcarpathian Oblast of Ukraine concerning the level of technological development have the potential to stimulate greater political action amongst the Rusyns. The following section will characterize the recent developments made in Ukraine and the possible outcomes of the contributions made by members of the Rusyn diaspora by means of the internet and EU legislation concerning minority rights.

According to Taras Kuzio, internet usage in Ukraine has consistently grown between thirty to forty percent, per year, over the past four years... making it the "most mobile medium and the least vulnerable to censorship."[348] This growth--stimulated by the recent reduction in computer prices and internet connection fees—has fostered an unpleasant political divide between the government and political opposition groups who now possess the technology to broadcast contrary viewpoints.[349] In the final months of 2001, the government "hired 3,000 computer experts" to the Security Service of Ukraine

---

[346] Ibid, page 5.

[347] From an article entitled, "Has 'Political Rusynism' Ended?" written by Jan Maksymiuk, in Radio Free Europe/Radio Liberty: Poland, Belarus, and Ukraine Report, Vol. 2, No.2, January 11, 2000. Also found at: http://www.rferl.org

[348] Kuzio, article entitled, "The Internet: Ukraine's New Samvydav," from 1/13/02, *The Ukrainian Weekly*, No2. Vol. LXX. Accessed online at: http://www.ukrweekly.com/Archive/2002/020204.shtml. Retrieved on March 3, 2004.

[349] Ibid. Kuzio suggests that there are 260 competing internet providers in Ukraine.

(SBU) as a way of limiting the number of anti-government websites and to gain greater control over the information being posted on the world wide web.[350]

But political opposition websites are only one aspect of government disapproval. The other "troubling" development is the increasing interconnectedness of Ukrainian society with their neighbors to the West. "Students and young people—among whom English is the most popular foreign language—are increasingly relying on the internet to conduct research as well as to read the Western media."[351] This reliance upon the English language poses a threat to the strength of the government of Ukraine because it is valued as the bridge to the West and more detrimental, Western democracy, freedom, and minority protection.

In Transcarpathia, where computer access has traditionally been limited, and the extension of the EU to its neighbors has made "crossing the border" more difficult, it has been the recent growth in "wireless communications" that has aided the Rusyns most dramatically. In fact, across Ukraine for two consecutive years the annual growth of consumers in wireless communication has been between 120%-140%, resulting in the type of stability U.S. firms find appealing.[352] The Industry Sector Analysis of Ukraine, published by the US Department of State in 2002, stated, "Ukraine is slowly emerging as a low cost site for high quality software development... and the national corporations have begun to engage in a price war that has allowed US companies to tap into an increasingly sophisticated network of agents and distributors throughout Ukraine who are able to reach a wide range of clients."[353] The production of wireless technology has resulted in certain areas of the Transcarpathia to move beyond the traditional process of computer development; one based on phone lines and determined band-width.

For Rusyns, however, much of this software and hardware is biased. "For maximum market penetration and exposure, US companies are advised to develop bilingual software (Ukrainian/Russian and English), as well as to provide the necessary bilingual written instructions and after-sales service."[354] The software, as mandated by the government of Ukraine is currently being developed in only the Ukrainian, Russian, and English languages because the Rusyn language is not recognized in Ukraine, and the Ruysn people lack marketability. Therefore, the Rusyns of Transcarpathia have had to rely on the internet and the wishes of their counterparts in countries entering the EU.

Cross-Border Democracy: The EU and Ukraine

Since 2002, there has been recent involvement from the European Union in the form of the Tacis Programme in Transcarpathia. Tacis Programmes are designed to offer "cross-border" solutions to non-EU member countries to help them gain greater self-sufficiency, provide support in the event of natural disasters, and attempt to establish liberal and open economic practices. The EU, and its desire to bring stability to all areas on the continent has entered the Transcarpathian Oblast through its most recent Tacis Programme, entitled, Pershyj KROK (First Step) as an attempt to bring "entrepreneurial

---

[350] Ibid.
[351] Ibid.
[352] Document published by the International Copyright, U.S. and Foreign Commercial Service and U.S. Department of State, 2002, entitled, "Trends in the ICT Market," Industry Sector Analysis of Ukraine.
[353] Ibid.
[354] Ibid.

skills to the people of Transcarpathia."[355] The Executive Director of the National Coordinating Unit of the Tacis Programme in Ukraine, Natalia Riabtseva stated that the desire of the EU is to "transform Ukraine into a democratic country with a market economy."[356] This "transformation" is perceived by the European Union as a way of establishing better economic participation in the east, and as a way of securing the dignity of the people of Transcarpathia who have continually been denied access to and respect from the government of Ukraine.

The government of Ukraine has suggested that these "cross border" solutions in Transcarpathia are in many ways obstructing its sovereignty and has continually threatened to leave the Tacis agreement.[357] Interestingly, it has not been the EU's advocacy for the development of entrepreneurial skills that has caused the greatest concern in Kiev, but rather the EU's emphasis on democratic freedoms and minority rights. In many ways the government in Kiev has begun to feel the pressure of the EU and its "march across the continent." Since the enhancement of Rusyn identity has been somewhat successful in other areas along the Subcarpathian Rus', now within the confines of the European Union, it is at least possible to assume that the government in Kiev fears that Rusyn autonomy is a distinct possibility due to the pressure of the EU and the increased level of foreign (primarily American) investment.

Urktelecom, and other former state-owned firms, seems to be losing the price war with Western IT (primarily American) firms. In many ways, the situation in Ukraine is parallel to that of Ireland before Irish accession into the EU. Although low, tax rates were not necessarily designed by the government of Ukraine, the privatization of certain major firms, the rise of the global economy, and a motivated work force has perpetuated an unprecedented level of high-tech growth and, since most of this growth is in the field of wireless mobile communications, foreign firms have begun to dominate Ukrainian society.[358] It is estimated that American investment represents about 25% of total foreign investment… a total that has increased annually by 46%.[359] Software producers such as the American firms Auriga and Telesystems "are now looking to take advantage of the highly skilled and inexpensive labor force in Ukraine."[360] "The labor market in Ukraine has a surplus of computer programmers, making it easy to find experts who can create sophisticated software products suitable for businesses located abroad, but at a fraction of the cost."[361] The economic development of Ukraine has created a strong Western influence and reliance upon the English language.

Although there is continuous speculation on a revival of Rusyn culture in Ukraine, a Western presence (economic and political) is bound to force a policy on the

---

[355] "The EU and Ukraine: News from the European Union's Cooperation Programme," February 2002, No. 21. Accessed at: http://www.inogate.org/pdf/news_2002Feb_en.pdf
[356] Ibid.
[357] Ibid.
[358] Department of State, "Trends in the ICT Market, " 2002.. "There are currently no domestic manufacturer of equipment for mobile communications networks in Ukraine; procurement needs are serviced by 12 foreign importers.
[359] Bougriy and Levsen, "Foreign Firms Push into Ukraine," *Business Information Service for the Newly Independent States*, accessed at: http:www.bisnis.doc.gov/bisnis/bulletin/9801push.htm. December 1997/January 1998.
[360] Andrea Curti, "Western Firms turn to Ukraine for Programmers," *Kiev Post*, June 23, 1998.
[361] Ibid.

admission of the distinctiveness of the Rusyn people. It is at this point time to conclude that the purpose of this case study was not to *prove* anything. It was merely intended to explore the possible relationship between the confluence of globalization with the response of the nation-state on the revival of the Rusyn identity. The background information, the examination of Rusyns in several countries within the EU, and the brief overview of developments in Ukraine, suggest that there exists some correlation between the European Union's emphasis on minority rights, the desire of the Eastern bloc to join the EU, and the rise in information technology on the Rusyn revival.

Conclusion

Although it appears that the process of globalization has caused a high degree of turbulence and chaos in the world, it does not appear that these processes have rendered the nation-state incapable of maintaining its sovereignty. Minority revival seems to be a result of globalization *and the continued power of the nation-state*. The ability of the European Union to promote and maintain a *European* culture within an economic model where survival is based upon productivity and conformity is evidence that the nation-state still matters.

The power and presence of the English language, the expanded responsibilities and initiatives of international organizations and non-governmental organizations, the high level of foreign direct investment, and the increased level in both the quality and accessibility of information technology have motivated nation-states to behave in unique ways. Although nation-states continue to assume the responsibility of creating policy, both foreign and domestic, they do so now in accordance with or in response to certain non-traditional sources of authority.

The processes of globalization have produced a paradox, one that has both expanded and contracted the traditional notions of European nationalism. The findings in this dissertation have suggested that there is a strong relationship between globalization and the elevation of minority nationalism within Europe. The recent social policies of the European Union based upon multilingualism and minority protection have elevated the awareness and status of minority nationalism, while diminishing the power and influence of "traditional" nationalism. For even if the notion of Carpatho-Rusyn nationalism is genuine, or at least *as genuine* as Russian or Ukrainian nationalism, its presence, notoriety, and accessibility are undeniably greater today than it has been in over a century.

Conversely, it is also now possible to assert that *traditional* nationalism has diminished as a result of the aforementioned process of globalization. This is a logical response to the concept of minority *revival*. As minority groups gain greater social and political protection as a result of the features of globalization, the nation-states have been pressured into policies that pertain to minority protection, i.e. traditional Italian, French, or Ukrainian nationalism has been weakened.

In this era of globalization, nation-states continue to play a large role in the world of "force and statecraft," yet the *fragmegration* of global society has changed allegiances and identities.[362] Nationalism, the source of both warfare and stability, the paradox of civil society, continues to grow and foster unity and division, however this time, in the name of democracy and human rights. The allowance of Slovene and Friulian nationalism in the Italian state is a good example of an unprecedented, European tolerance towards minority communities.

Although certain traditional nationalists continue to assault the "authenticity" of the nationalism of the minority group, the current era has allowed the minorities to gain a certain amount of cohesion and visibility. The presence and influence of Magocsi in the literature of Carpatho-Rusynism is unavoidable. Yet even if Magocsi *is directly*

---

[362] The phrase "force and statecraft" refers to the book by Craig and George of the same name. "Fragmegration" refers to the concept presented by Rosenau.

responsible for the increased awareness of the Carpatho-Rusyns, it is this era of globalization that has afforded him greater exposure and freedom.

In closing, I feel it my responsibility to address future considerations. While I do not believe that the nation-states of Europe, both east and west, are in immediate danger of being overthrown, I do believe that the notion of sovereignty has shifted from the national to the supranational. I also believe that the European Union will continue to increase its role in global security and economic exchange. Open passage and economic standardization has allowed the local minorities to speak the English language and to partake in a political and economic system based not on loyalty to the *nationalism* of the nation-state, but the loyalty to liberalization and democracy. If the governments of Europe continue to standardize, they will not witness a reduction in the level of nationalism, but an increase, because the word "European" will become more important yet also, at the same time, equal to the believed identity of anyone that dwells upon the continent. In essence, the revival of linguistic communities throughout Europe is due to both globalization and politics. Thus politics still matters in language revival.

Bibliography

Achard, Pierre. "Discours et Sociologie du langage," *Langage et Societie*, No. 37, pp.5-61, 1986.

Alatas, Syed H., and Hussein Alatas. *Myth of the Lazy Native*, Frank Cass and Co. 1977.

Alfredsson, Gudmundur. "Report on Equality and Non-Discrimination: Minority Rights," Strasbourg: Councilof Europe, 1990.

Allen, Kieran. *The Celtic Tiger: The Myth of Social Partnership in Ireland*, Manchester University Press, 2000.

Antimoon.com. Accessed on March 13, 2004.

Armstrong, Warwick. "Culture, Continuity, and Identity in the Slovene-Italian Border Region," in Anderson,et. al (eds) Culture and Cooperation in Europe's Borderlands, European Studies 19, pp. 145-170.

Anderson, Benedict. *Imagined Communities: Reflections on the Origin and Spread of Nationalism.* London: Verso Books, 1991.

Applegate, Celia. "A Europe of Regions: Reflections on the Historiography of Sub-National Places in ModernTimes," *The American Historical Review*, vol. 104, no.4, pp. 1157-1182.

Aspinwall, Mark and Gerald Schneider. "Same Menu, Separate Tables: The Institutionalist Turn in Political Science and the Study of European Integration." in *The Rulesof Integration: The Institutionalist Approach to European Studies*, edited by Mark Aspinwall and Gerald Schneider. Manchester: Manchester University Press, 2000.

Avalon Project at Yale University Law School. *A Compilation of the Messages and Papers of the Presidents*, prepared under the direction of the Joint Committee on printing of the House and Senate. Pursuant to an Act of the 52nd Congress of the United States. New York: Bureau of National Literature, Inc. 1897. Accessed here from: http://www.yale.edu/lawweb/avalon/presiden/messages/tj006.htm December 12, 2003.

Baker, Stephen, Inka Resch, Kate Carlisle, and Katharine A.Schmidt. "The Great English Divide," *Businessweek Online*, August 13, 2001.

Ballinger, Pamela. *History in Exile: Memory and Identity at the Borders of the Balkans*, Princeton University Press, 2003.

Ballo, Aron. "Hungarian government to spend nearly 4 million euros setting up Transylvanian Hungarian in Romania, meanwhile language discrimination continues," from Eurolang.net (http://www.eurolang.net) Accessed on February 26, 2004

Bally, Charles and Albert Sechehaye (eds) *Ferdinand de Saussure's, Course in General Linguistics*, London, Duckworth Publishing, 1983.

Barber, Benjamin R. and Andrea Schulz. *Jihad vs. McWorld: How Globalism and Tribalism is Reshaping the World*, Ballantine Books, Reprint Edition, 1996.

Biersteker, Thomas J, and Rodney Bruce Hall (eds). *The Emergence of Private Authority in Global Governance*, Cambridge University Press, 2003

Bindas, D. "Ruske Nar. Prosvitne Druztvo," *Ruske Novini*, Number 234, Novi Sad, 1929, pp. 2.

Borkanjuk, Oleksa. *Who are we and where do we belong?*, Uzhorod, 1937.

93

Bougriy, Maxim and Shawn Levsen. "Foreign Firms Push into Ukraine," Business Information Service for the Newly Independent States. Accessed at: http://bisnis.doc.gov/bisnis/bulletin/9801push.htm. December 1997/January 1998.

Bradley, John. "The Irish economy in international perspective," Chapter 3 of Crotty and Schmidt's (eds), *Ireland on the World Stage*, Longman Publishing Group, pp. 46-65, 2002.

Breton, Roland J. *Atlas of the Languages and Ethnic Communities of South Asia*. New Delhi: Sage Publications, 1997.

Bringa, Tone. *Being Musilim the Bosnian Way: Identity and Community in a Central Bosnian Village*, Princeton University Press, 1995.

Brown, David. *Contemporary Nationalism: Civic, Ethnocultural, and Multicultural Politics*. New York: NY, Routledge Press, 2000.

Bryson, Bill. *The Mother Tongue: English and How It Got That Way*, William Morrow, 1996.

Burbach, Roger and William Robinson. "The Fin de Siecle Debate: Globalization as an Epochal Shift," *Science and Society*, Vol. 63, No. 1, Spring 1999, pp. 10-39.

Calleo, David. *Rethinking Europe's Future*. Princeton University Press, 2001.

Camillieri, Joseph A. and James Falk. The *End of Sovereignty? The Politics of a Shrinking and Fragmenting World*. Aldershot: Edward Elgar Publishing, 1992.

Carpathian Connection, The. Found at: http://www.tccweb.org.

Castells, Manuel. *The Information Age: Economy, Society, and Culture*, Blackwell Publishers, 1999.

Chalupa, Andrea. "The People from the Borderlands," *The Slovak Spectator*, Vol.10, No.5, February 19-15, 2004.

Checkel, Jeffrey L. "Bridging the Rational Choice/Constructivist Gap? Theorizing Social Interaction in European Institutions" *Arena Working Papers*, WP 00/11, May 15, 2000. Found at: http://www.arena.uio.no/publications/wp00_11.htm

Choi, Changkyu. "Does the Internet stimulate inward foreign direct investment?" *Journal of Policy Modeling*, Vol. 25, Iss.4, pp. 319-326, June 2003.

Cobo, Jose R. Martinez. "Study of the Problem of Discrimination against Indigenous Populations," United Nations Document: E/CN.4/Sub.2/1986/7/Add.4/1986, p. 29.

Coe, Cati. "Educating an African Leadership: Achimota and the Teaching of African Culture in the Gold Coast," in *Africa Today*, Volume 49, Issue 3, 2002.

Cohn, Theodore H., Stephen McBride, and John Richard Wiseman. *Power in theGlobal Era: Grounding Globalization*, Palgrave Macmillan, 2000.

Collins, Valerie. "Clinging to Life." Found at: http://www.spainview.com/valerieclinging.html. Accessed on August 16, 2003.

Colonna, Fanny. *Instituteurs Algerians: 1883-1939*, Paris: Travaux Recherches de Science Politique, no. 36, 1975.

Columbia International Affairs Online. Working paper entitled, "Ethnic Identity, Historical Memory, and Nationalism in Post Soviet States," Found at: http://www.ciaonet.org/wps/pra)1/index.html. Accessed on August 16, 2003.

Coluzzi, Paolo. "Regional and Minority Languages in Italy: A general introduction on the present situation and acomparison of 2 case studies: Milanese and Friulian," Working Paper 14, from Mercator's Working Papers collection found at, http://www.ciemen.org/mercator/pdf/wp14-def-ang.pdf, 2004.

Committee of the Regions. Accessible online at: http://ica.cordis.lu.

Commons, J.R. *Races and Immigrants in America.* Augustus M.Kelly Publishers, 1967.

Constitution of the French Republic of 1958. Article I and Article II.

Coolidge, Louis. *An Old Fashioned Senator: Orville H. Platt of Connecticut, The Story of a Life Unselfishly Devoted to the Public Service,* Kennikat Press, 1910.

CORDIS Project. Accessible online at: http://ica.cordis.lu.

Cosolo, Andrew. "The State of Friulian Today and Tomorrow," found online at: http://www.geocities.com/Athens/Styx/9982/today.htm

Cox, Beth. "U.S. Internet dominance waning," E-   Commerceguide.com, April 11, 2000. Found online at: http://ecommerce.internet.com/news/insights/trends/article/0,3371,10417_338521 00.html

Craig, Gordan A. and Alexander L. George. *Force and Statecraft,* Fourth Edition, New York: NY, Oxford University Press, 1995.

Cruciato, Paolo. Interview on October 12, 2003.

Crystal, David. *English as a Global Language,* Second Edition, New York: Cambridge University Press, 2003

Crystal, David. *Language and the Internet,* New York: Cambridge University Press, 2001.

Curti, Andrea. "Western Firms into Ukraine for Programmers," *Kiev Post,* June 23, 1998.

Cutler, A. Claire, Virginia Haufler, and Tony Porter (eds). "The Contours and Significance of Private Authority in International Affairs," Chapter 12 of their book entitled, *Private Authority and International Affairs,*1999.

Das Gupta, D. Linguistic Studies in Juang, Kharia Tar, Lodha, Mal-Pariyha, Ghatoali, Pahariya. Anthropological Survey of India, Calcutta.

Delanty, Gerard. "The Resurgence of the City in Europe? The Spaces of European Citizenship," in Isin (ed) Democracy, Citizenship, and the Global City, pp. 79-92, 2000.

Drucker, Peter F. *Post-Capitalist Society,* Harper Business, Reprint Edition, 1994.

Duc'-Fajfer, Olena. "The Lemkos of Poland," Chapter 3 of *The Persistence of Regional Cultures,* edited by Paul Robert Magocsi, 1993, pp. 83-104.

DuMont, Marya. "Minority Sociolinguistics in Europe: The Occitan Language Versus The French State," Master of Arts Thesis, University of Chicago, 1996. Found at: http://tuna.uchicago.edu/homes/marya/MAThesisnotes.html. Accessed on March 1, 2003.

Durant, Will and Ariel Durant. *The Story of Civillization, Part VII: The Age of   Reason Begins,* Simon and Schuster, 1961.

Echeruo, Michael. "The Education of Lagosians," West Africa Review, 2001.

Economist, The. "Language and electronics: the coming global tongue," pp. 37, December 21, 1996.

Economist, The. "The Other Government in Bangladesh," July 25, 1998.

Edwards, Michael and David Hulme. *Beyond the Magic Bullet Non-Governmental Organizations—Performance and Accountability*, Kumarian Press, 1996.

Enriquez, Virgilio G. *Neocolonial Politics and the Language Struggle in the Philippines: National Consciousness and Language in Philippine Psychology, 1971-1983*, Philippine Psychology Research and Training House, 1989.

Erickson, Jim. "Cyberspeak: the death of diversity," *Asiaweek*, pp. 15, July 3, 1998.

Eurolang. Accessed online at http://www.eurolang.net.

Euromosaic. Profile of the Friulian Language. Found at: http://www.uoc.edu/euromosaic/web/document/friula/an/i1/il/html#2

Euromosaic. Found at: http://www.uoc.edu/euromosaic/web/document/esolve/an/i 1/il.htm

European Bureau for Lesser Used Languages. "About Us," webpage found online at: http:www.eblul.org. Accessed on August 23, 2003.

EBLUL, Annex A.2: "Introduction to the Draft Work Programme 03-04." Accessed from: http://ww2.eblul.org:8080/eblul/Public/projets_en_cours/priorities_and_resul8772/view. Found on February26, 2004.

EBLUL. Report on Minorities: Slovenes in Italy, 2001-2003.

European Union. "Structural Funds:Commission contributes three million euros to program of innovative action in the region of Friuli Venezia-Giulia, 2002-2003. Found at: http://europa.eu.int/comm/regional_policy/innovation/p df/programme/frioulivenezia_en.pdf.

European Commission Directorate General for Education and Culture. "Europe Unties Tongues," from *The Magazine: Education and Culture in Europe*, Issue 22, 2004. Accessed online at: http://europa.eu.int/comm/dgs/education_culture/mag/22/en.pdf

European Union Cooperate Programme. "The EU and Ukraine: News from the EU's Cooperation Programme," No. 21, February 2002. Found at: http://www.inogate.org/pdf/news_2002Feb_en.pdf

Feis, Herbert. *From Trust to Terror: The Onset of the Cold War, 1945-1950*, W.W. Norton and Co., 1970.

Filevic, Ivan. *Iz storii Karpatskoj Rusi: Ocerki Galicko-russkoj ziznis 1772*, Warsaw, 1972.

Filippucci, Paola. "Anthropological Perspectives of Culture in Italy," in Forgacs and Lumley (eds), *Italian Cultural Studies: An Introduction*, pp. 52-71, 1996.

Fishman, Joshua (ed). *Readings in the Sociology of Language*. The Hague, Mouten, 1968.

------------------------*The Sociology of Language: An Interdisciplinary Social Science Approach to Language in Society*. Rowley: MA, Newbury House Publishers, 1972.

Forgacs, David and Robert Lumley (eds) *Italian Cultural Studies: An Introduction*, Oxford University Press, 1996.

Friedman, Thomas. *Longitudes and Attitudes: The World in The Age of Terrorism*, Anchor Books/Doubleday, 2003.

Gaetano, Pietro. Interview, October 16, 2003.

Gellner, Ernest. *Nations and Nationalism*. Ithaca, NY: Cornell University Press, 1983.

------------------*Culture, Identity, and Politics*. New York: NY, Cambridge: Cambridge University Press, 1987.

----------------- *Encounters with Nationalism*. Blackwell Publishers, 2002.

Giddens, Anthony. *Runaway World: How Globalization is Reshaping Our Lives*, Profile Books, 1999.

Giuricin, Gianni. *Trieste: Luci e Ombre*, Trieste: Tabographis, 1988.

Global Reach. "Global Internet Statistics of 2003," Found at: http://www.glreach.com/globstats. Accessed March 2, 2004.

Glyn, Andrew and Bob Sutcliffe. "Global but Leaderless? The New Capitalist Order," in Milliband and Panitch's (eds), *The New World Order: The Socialist Register*, Merlin Press, pp. 76-95, 1992.

Goody, Jack. *The Logic of Writing and the Organization of Society*. New York: NY, Cambridge University Press, 1987.

Gottlieb, Gidon. "Nations without States," *Foreign Affairs*, Vol. 73, No. 3, May/June, 1994.

Gross, David A. "The digital dimension of development," *Global Issues: The Evolving Internet* (Electronic Journal of the United States Department of State), Volume 8, Number 3, November 2003.

Hall, John A. *The State of the Nation*. New York: NY, Cambridge University Press, 2000.

Hancock, M. Donald, and B. Guy Peters. "What is the Future of EU Politics," Chapter 35 of the book, *Politics in Europe*, Third Edition, edited by Hancock, Conradt, et al., Chatham House Publishers of Seven Bridges Press, 2003.

Hassanpour, Amir. "The Politics of A-political Linguistics, LinguistsandLinguicide." Found in Rights to Language, Equity, Power, and Education, Celebrating the 60th Birthday of Tove Skutnabb-Kangas, Edited by Robert Phillipson, Published by Lawrence Erlbaum Associates, 2000.

Haugen, Einar. "Language Planning in Modern Norway." Found in *Scandinavian Studies 33*, 1961.

Hawisher, Gail E. and Cynthia L. Slefe (eds). *Global Literacies and the Worldwide Web*, Routledge, 1999.

Heady, Patrick. *Hard People: Rivalry, Sympathy, and Social Structure in an Alpine Valley*, The Netherlands: Overseas Publishing Association, 1999.

Heine, Bernd and Derek Nurse (eds). *African Languages: An Introduction*, Cambridge University Press, 2000.

Held, David, Anthony G. McGrew, David Goldblatt, and Jonathon Perraton (eds). *Global Transformations: Politics, Economics and Culture*, Stanford University Press, 1999.

Held, David. "Democracy and Globalization," Working Paper from the Max Planck Institute for the Study of Societies, May 1997.

Holmes, Douglas. *Integral Europe: Fast-Capitalism, Multiculturalism, Neo-Fascism*, Princeton University Press, 2000.

Holmes, Douglas R. and Jean Quataert. "An approach to modern labor: worker peasantries in historic Saxony and the Friuli region over three centuries," *Comparative Studies in Sociology and History*, Vol.28, No.2, pp. 191-216, April

1986.

Hooghe, Liesbet and Gary Marks. *Multilevel Governance and European Integration,* Rowman and Littlefield Publishers, 2001.

Hroch, Miroslav. Chapter entitled, "Real and Constructed: the nature of nations." Found in *The State of The Nation: Ernest Gellner and The Theory of Nationalism,* edited by John A. Hall. New York: NY, Cambridge University Press, 2000.

Huang, Douglas. Computer Usage Survey from *Magellan's Log.* Found at: http://texaschapbookpress.com/computerusagecomplete.htm.

Hungarian Constitution. Article 68.

Huntington, Samuel. "Clash of Civilizations," *Foreign Affairs, Agenda 1994,* pp. 122.

Huss, Leena, Antoinette Camilleri Grima, Kendall King, et. al. (eds). *Transcending Monolingualism: Linguistic Revitalization in Education,* Ashgate Publishing, 2003.

International Copyright United States and Foreign Commercial Service and U.S. Department of State. "Trends in the ICT Market: Industry Sector Analysis of Ukraine, 2002.

International Institute for Strategic Studies. *The Military Balance, 2002-2003,* International Institute for Strategic Studies, Book and Map edition, 2002.

International Monetary Fund. "The Information Technology Revolution," found in *World Economic Outlook,* October 2001.

Intriligator, Michael. "Globalization of the World Economy: Potential benefits and costs and a net assessment," Paper presented at the Instituto Affari Internazionali on "Governing Stability Across the Mediterranean Sea: A Trans-Atlantic Perspective," March 21-23, 2003 in Rome, Italy.

Italian Language Law 482/1999.

ISTAT. Census data of 2000.

Jenkins, S. "The Triumph of English," *The Times of London,* February 25, 1995.

Jurkowski, Marian. "Lemkowszczyzna: materially do bibliografii," *Slavia Orientalis,* 5, Warsaw, 1962, pp. 525-536.

Kaldor, Mary. *New and Old Wars: Organized Violence in a Global Era,* Stanford University Press, 1999.

Kann, Robert. *The Multinational Empire: Nationalism and National Reform in the Hapsburg Monarchy, 1848-1914,* Vols. I and II, NY: Octagon Press, 1977.

Keating, Michael. *Plurinational Democracy: Stateless Nations in a Post-Sovereignty Era,* Oxford University Press, 2002.

---------------------*State and Regional Nationalism: Territorial Politics and the European State,* Hemel Hempstead: Harvester Wheatsheaf, 1988.

Kelman, H. "Language as an Aid and Barrier to Involvement in the National System." Found in *Can Language Be Planned,* edited by Joan Rubin and Bjorn H. Jernudd, University of Hawaii Press, 1971.

Kemper, Cynthia. "Sacre Bleu! English as a Global Lingua Franca? Why English is achieving worldwide status," *Communication World,* June/July 1999, Vol. 16, Iss.6, pp. 41-44.

Kent, Roland G. "The Sounds of Latin: A descriptive and historical phonology," *Language*, Vol.8, No. 3, Waverly Press, pp. 11-216, 1932.

Kirby, Peadar. *The Celtic Tiger in Distress: Growth with Inequality in Ireland*, Palgrave MacMillan, 2002.

Kohn, Hans. *The Idea of Nationalism: A Study in its Origins and Background*. New York: NY, Macmillan Publishing Co., 1967.

Krasner, Stephen. "Sovereignty," from Chapter One of *Global Politics in a Changing World* by Richard W. Mansbach and Edward J. Rhodes, Houghton Mifflin College, 2000.

Kreitor, Nikolai von, "American Political Theology," from *Archivo Eurasia*, at http://utenti.lycos.it/ArchivEurasia/kreitor_apt.html on December 22, 2003.

Kuzio, Taras. "The Internet: Ukraine's New Samvydav," *The Ukrainian Weekly*, No.2, Vol.LXX, January 13, 2002.
http://www.ukrweekly.com/Archive/2002/020204.shtml

Lamb, David. *The Africans*, Vintage Press, 1984.

Laun, Karen M., "A Fractured Identity: The Lemko of Poland," *Central Europe Review*, December 5, 1999.

Liddell, A.C. "Introduction," to Defoe's, *The Life and Adventures of Robinson Crusoe*, Oxford: Clarendon Press, 1910.

Lipson, Leslie. *The Great Issues of Politics*. Second Edition. Prentice-Hall, 1965.

Lundestad. G. "Why does globalization encourage fragmentation?" *International Politics*, June 2004, Vol. 41, No.2, pp. 265-276.

Macartney, C.A. *National States and National Minorities*, Oxford University Press, 1934.

Macauley, Thomas. "Minute on Indian Education," in Clive and Pinney's (eds), *Thomas Babington Macauley: Selected Writings*, Chicago: University of Chicago Press, 1972.

Machiavelli, Niccolo. The Prince, Bantam Books, Re-Issue edition, 1984.

Mackerras, Colin. *Western Images of China*, Hong Kong: Oxford University Press, 1989.

Macionis, John J. Sociology, Fifth edition. Prentice Hall Publishers, 2002.

Mac Sherry, Ray, and Padraic A White. *The Making of the Celtic Tiger: The Inside Story of Ireland's Boom   Economy*, Mercier Press, 2000.

Magocsi, Paul R. *Carpatho-Rusyn Studies: An Annotated Bibliography, Volume I, 1975-1984*, Columbia University Press, 1988.

--------------------"Made or Re-made in America? Nationality and Identity Formation Among Carpatho-Rusyn Immigration and Their Descendants," in *The Persistence of Regional Cultures*, Columbia University Press,1993, pp.163-174.

--------------------"Mapping Stateless Peoples: The East Slavs of the Carpathians," *Canadian Slavic Papers*, XXXIX, 3-4, Edmonton, 1999, pp. 301-331.

--------------------"The End of the Nation-State: The Revolutions of 1989 and the Future of Europe," Chapter 38 on the book, *Of the Making of Nationalities, There is No End*, Volume II by Paul Robert Magocsi. East European Monographs, Columbia University Press, 1999, pp.306-320.

--------------------*The Language Question Among the Subcarpathian Rusyns*, Carpatho-Rusyn Research Center, 1979.

--------------------(ed) *The Persistence of Regional Cultures*, Columbia University Press, 1993.

--------------------*The Rusyns of Slovakia, An Historical Survey*, Classics of Carpatho-Rusyn Scholarship, Vol. VI, Columbia University Press, 1993.

--------------------*The Rusyn Question*, found online at: http://litopys.narod.ru/rizne/magocie.htm

--------------------"The Ruthenian Decision to Unite with Czecholslovakia," *Slavic Review*, Vol. 34, No.2, June 1975, pp. 360-385.

--------------------*The Shaping of National Identity: Subcarpathian Rus', 1848-1948*, Cambridge: Harvard University Press, 1978.

Mair, Christian (ed). *The Politics of English as a World Language: New Horizons Post-Colonial Cultural Studies, Cross/Cultures 65*, Rodopi Publishing, 2003.

Maksymiuk, Jan. "Has 'Political Rusynism' Ended?" *Radio Free Europe/Radio Liberty: Poland, Belarus, and Ukraine Report*, Vol.2, No.2, January 11, 2000. http://www.rferl.org

Mangan, J.A. *The Games Ethic and Imperialism: Aspects of the Diffusion of an Ideal*, Harmondsworth: Viking Press, 1985.

Manow, Philip. "Globalization, corporate finance, and coordinated capitalism: Pension finance in Germany and Japan," a working paper from the Max Plank Institutefor the Study of Societies. August 2001. Found at: http://www.ciaonet.org/wps/map06/index.html

Mansbach, Richard and Edward Rhodes (eds). *Global Politics in a Changing World*, Houghton Mifflin, 2000.

Maranelli, Carlo and Gaetano Salvemini. *Questione dell'Adriatico*, Rome: Libreria della Voce, 1918.

Marinelli, Giovanni. *Slavi, Tedeschi, Italiani, nel Cosidetto (Littorale) Austriaco (Istria, Trieste, Gorizia)*, Venice: Antonelli Publishers, 1885.

Massad, Joseph A. *Colonial Effects: The Making of National Identity in Jordan*, Columbia University Press, 2001.

Matsuzawa, "New Dictionary for New Times," *The Yomiuri Shimbun*, September 30, 2003.

Matvey, David. "Ruthenian language rights take one big step forward, a half step back in Slovakia, while Slovakia takes a big step forward," *Rusyn News and Information Service*. Http://www.legacyrus.com/NewsReel/RusynNews/SlovakLanguageLawPasses.html

Mauro, Max. "Multilingual region Friuli Venezia-Giulia to include linguistic rights in legal revision," *Organizzazione per la Minoranze Europee*, April 26, 2004. Found at: http://www.eurominority.org/version/it/actualitedetail.asp.

Medjesi, Ljubomir. "The Problem of Cultural Borders in the History of Ethnic Groups: The Yugoslav Rusyns," Chapter Five of the edited work of Paul Robert Magocsi entitled, *The Persistence of Regional Cultures*, Columbia University Press, 1993, pp.139-162.

Messina, Anthony M. and Colleen V. Thouez. "The Logic and Politics of a European Immigration Regime," Chapter 5 of Messina's (ed) *Western European Immigrant Policy in the New Century*, 2002.

Michalski, Anna and Helen Wallace. *The European Community: The Challenge of Enlargement*, London: Royal Institute of International Affairs, 1992.

Miller, Kerby. *Emigrants and Exiles: Ireland and Irish Exodus to North America*. New York: NY, Oxford University Press, 1988.

Miller, Kerby and Patricia Mulholland Miller. *Journey of Hope: The Story of Irish Immigration to America*. San Francisco: CA, Chronicle Books, 2001.

Milliband, Ralph and Leo Panitch (eds). *The New World Order? The Socialist Register*, London: Merlin Press, 1992.

Minnich, Robert Gary. "The individual as author of collective identities: reconsidering identity formations within a multilingual community," from the edited book entitled, *Multilingualism on European Borders - The Case of Val Canale*, Edited by Irena and Salvatore Venosi, pp.159-175, Slovene Research Institute, 1996.

Misra, Maria. "Lessons of Empire: Britain and India," *SAIS Review*, Vol.23, No.2, Johns Hopkins Press, 2003.

Moravcsik, Andrew. "Is Something Rotten in the State of Denmark? Constructivism and European Integration." *Journal of European Public Policy* 6 (Special Issue): 669-681, 1999.

Motyl, Alexander J. *Nations, Empires, and Revolutions: Conceptual Limits and Theoretical Possibilities*. New York: NY, Columbia University Press, 1999.

Murphy, Antoin E. "The 'Celtic Tiger'—An analysis of Ireland's economic growth performance." A working paper from the Robert Schuman Center for Advanced Studies, RSC 2000/16, 2000.

Musynka, Mykola. "The Postwar Development of the Regional Culture of the Rusyn-Ukrainians of Czechoslovakia," Chapter 2 of Magocsi's book entitled, *The Persistence of Regional Cultures*, Columbia University Press, 1993, pp. 53-82.

Mysanyc, Oleska V. "From Subcarpathian Rusyns to Transcarpathian Ukrainians," from the book entitled, *The Persistence of Regional Cultures*, edited by Paul Robert Magocsi, 1993, pp. 7-52.

Nairn, Tom. Chapter entitled, "The curse of rurality: limits of modernization theory." Found in *The State of The Nation: Ernest Gellner and The Theory of Nationalism*, edited by John A. Hall. New York: NY, Cambridge University Press, 2000.

Nations of the World: A Political, Economic, and Business Handbook, Greyhouse Publishing, 2003.

Nikolas, Margareta Mary. "False Opposites in Nationalism: An Examination of the Dichotomy of Civic Nationalism in Modern Europe." Master of Art's Thesis at The Center for European Studies, Monash University, 1999.

Norris, Pippa. *Digital Divide: Civic Engagement, Information Poverty, and the Internet Worldwide*, Cambridge University Press, 2001.

Novak, Bogdan. *Trieste, 1941-1954: The Ethnic, Political, and Ideological Struggle*, University of Chicago Press, 1970.

Ohannessian, Sirarpi, and Mubanga E. Kashoki (eds). *Language in Zambia*, London: International African Institute, 1978.

Ohmae, Kenichi. *The Borderless World*, Harper Collins, 1990.

O'Riain, Sean. "The Flexible Developmental State: Globalization, Information Technology, and the Celtic Tiger," *Politics and Society*, Vol. 28, No.2, pp. 157- 193, June 2000.

O'Riain, Sean and Philip J. "The role of the state in growth and welfare," in the book edited by Nolan, O'Connell, and Whelan (eds) entitled, *Bust to Boom? The Irish Experience of Growth and Inequality*, Dublin: Institute of Public Administration, 2000.

Outpost Dispatch: Newsletter of Rusyn Outpost North America. August 23, 2003.

Pattanayak, D. P. *Mutilingualism and Mother-Tongue Education*, Oxford University Press, 1981.

Pennycook, Alistair. *The Cultural Politics of English as an International Language*, Addison-Wesley Publishing, 1994.

Phillipson, Robert. *Linguistic Imperialism*, New York: Oxford University Press, 1992.

Pimental, Benjamin. "Images of Racism: How 19th Century U.S. Media Depicted Filipinos, and Other Non-whites as Savages," *San Francisco Chronicle*, July 17, 2001.

Pizzi, Katia. "Birth of a Nation: The National Question in Vamba's, *Giornalino della Domenica*, 1906-1911," Paper presented at the International Research Society for Children's Literature, August 2001. Found at: http://www.childlit.org.za/irsclpappizzi.html

Poland Development Gateway. Found at http://www.pldg.pl/p/en/nw/2762

Pozun, Brian. "The Rusyns of Hungary: End of The Millenial Struggle," *Central Europe Review*, Vol. 3, No. 16, May 7, 2001.

----------------"Trieste's Burden of History," *Central Europe Review*, Vol.3, No.6, February 12, 2001.

----------------"News from Slovenia," *Central Europe Review*, Vol.3, No.7, February 19, 2001.

Priestly, Tom. "The Position of the Slovenes in Austria: Recent Developments in Political and Other Attitudes," *Nationalities Papers*, March 1999, Vol.27, Iss.1, pp. 103-114.

Prozauskas, Algis. "Ethnic Identity, Historical Memory, and Nationalism in Post Soviet States." Working Paper from the Center for Studies of Social Change, March, 1995.Accessed on August 16, 2003 from Columbia International Online Affairs at: www.ciaonet.org/

Rafael, Vicente L. "Regionalism, Area Studies, and the Accidents of Agency," *The American Historical Review*, vol. 104, no. 4, October 1999, pp. 1208-1220.

Regional Law 5 of Friuli Venezia-Giulia, 1996

Regional Law 11 of Friuli Venezia-Giulia, Italy, 1969.

Reinfuss, Roman. "Stan I problematyka badan nad kultura lodowa Lemkowsczyzna," *Etnografia Polska*, 5, Warsaw, Wroclaw, and Krakow, 1961, pp. 63-68.

Republic of Slovenia: Ministry of Education, Science and Sport. Accessible at: http://www.mszs.si/eng/ministry/publications/development/pogl_03.asp

Reynolds, Matthew J. "Rusyn Patriots Questioning Purpose of Linguistic Revival," *The Slovak Spectator*. Found at: http://www.tccweb.org/rusynback.htm March 2, 2004.

Ricca, Angelo. Interview of October 13, 2003.

Richie, J.A. (ed) *Selections from Educational Records, Part II: 1840-1859*, from the Bureau of Education (Britain), Calcutta: Superintendent of Government Printing, 1922.

Robbins, Richard H. *Global Problems and the Culture of Capitalism*, Allyn and Bacon, 2001.

Rogel, Carole. *The Slovenes and Yugoslavism*, Columbia University Press, 1977.

------------------*The Breakup of Yugoslavia and Its Aftermath: Revised Edition*, Greenwood Press, 2004.

Rosenau, James. *Turbulence in World Politics: Theory of Change and Continuity*, Princeton University Press, 1990.

--------------------*Along the Foreign-Domestic Frontier: Exploring Governance in a Turbulent World*, Cambridge University Press, 1997.

Rot, Alexander. "Josef Dobrovskij o jazyke zakarpatskich ukraincev," *Naukovi Zapysky Uzhorods'koho derzavnoho universytetu*, IX, Uzhorod, 1954, pp. 254-260.

Rudolph, Joseph. "Ethnic sub-states and the emergent politics of tri-level interaction in Western Europe," *Western Political Quarterly*, Vol. 30, No.4, December 1977.

Rusinow, Dennison. *Italy's Austrian Heritage, 1919-1946*, Oxford University Press, 1966.

Sampat, Payal. "Last Words," *World Watch*, Volume 14, Number 3, May/June 2001.

Sassen, Saskia. *The Global City: New York, Tokyo, and London*, Princeton University Press, 2001.

------------------"The Participation of States and Citizens in Global Governance," *Indiana Journal of Global Legal Studies*, Winter 2003, Vol.10, Iss.1, pp.5-28.

Scencic, Alex. Interview of October 11, 2003.

Sedelmeir, Ulrich and Helen Wallace. "Eastern Enlargement," Chapter 16 of the book, *Policymaking in the European Union*, Fourth Edition, edited by Helen and William Wallace, Oxford University Press, 2000, pp.427-460.

Seite, B., D. Bachut, D. Maret, and B. Roudad. "Presentation of the Eurolang Project," Funded by the SITE Corporation, from the Proclamation of Coling-92, in Nantes. Presented August 23-28, 1992. Found online at: http://acl.ldc.upenn.edu/C/C92/C92-4209.pdf

Seton-Watson, Robert W. "Preface" in *Europe in the Melting Pot*, London: MacMillan and Co., 1919.

Shin, Gi-Wook. "The paradox of Korean globalization," Working Paper from the Asia Pacific Research Center at Stanford University, January 2003.

Shils, Edward. *The Intellectuals and the Powers, and Other Essays*, Chicago: University of Chicago Press, 1972.

Shonfield, Andrew. *Modern Capitalism*, Oxford University Press, 1965.

Simons, Marlise. "Old European Tongues Flourish in Revival of Regional Cultures," *New York Times, International Section*, October 17, 1999.

Simpson, John A. (ed.) *Oxford English Dictionary*. Oxford Press, 2002.

Skutnabb-Kangas, Tove. *Linguistic Genocide in Education—Or   Worldwide Diversity and Human Rights?* Lawrence Erlbaum Associates, Inc., 2000.

Skutnabb-Kangas, Tove et.al. (eds) *Linguistic Human Rights:Overcoming Linguistic Discrimination*, Walter de Gruyter, Inc., 1995.

Sloane, Sarah, and Jason Johnstone. "Reading sideways, backwards, and across: Scottish and American literacy practices and weaving the web," chapter 7 of *Global Literacy and The World Wide Web*, edited by Hawisher and Selfe, Routledge: 1999, pp.154-186.

Slovene Language Technologies Society. Accessible at: http://nl.ijs.si/sdjt/sdjt-www-e en.html#institutions

Stourzh, Gerard. "Ethnic Attribution in Late Imperial Austria: Good Intentions, Evil Consequences," in Robertson and Timms, *The Hapsburg Legacy*, pp.70-75.

Sluga, Glenda. *The Problem of Trieste and the Italo-Yugoslav Border: Difference, Identity, and Sovereignty in 20th Century Europe*, State University of New York Press, 2001.

Soysal, Yasemin Nuhoglu. *Limits of Citizenship: Migrants and Post National Membership in Europe,* University of Chicago Press, 1994.

Sweeney, Paul. *The Celtic Tiger: Ireland's Continuing Economic Miracle*, Oak Tree Press, 2000.

Sysyn, Frank. "On Lemko Identity," from Magocsi's edited book, *Of the Making of Nationalities: There is no end*, Volume II, pp. 113-137, 1999.

Tallon, Paul and Kenneth L. Kraemer. "Information Technology and Economic Development: Ireland's Coming of Age with Lessons for Developing Countries," Working Paper presented at the 32nd Hawaii International Conference on System Sciences. Found online at: www.crito.uci.edu.

Taylor, Charles. "Nationalism and Modernity." Found in Chapter eight of *The State of The Nation*, edited by John A. Hall. New York: NY, Cambridge University Press, 2000.

Tedeschi, Giuseppe. Interview of October 12, 2003.

Temporale, Christian. "Pier Paolo Pasolini: His Life," Found online at: http://www.pasolini.net/english_bigraphia01.htm. Accessed March 4, 2004.

Thiesse, Anne-Marie. "Democracy softens forces of change: Inverting national identity," *Le Monde Diplomatique*, Found at: http//:www.globalpolicy.org/national/identity.htm.

Tichy, Frantisek. "Josef Dobrovsky a Podkarpatska Rus," in Josef Dobrovsky sbornik stati, Prague, 1929, pp. 332- 343.

Tonel, Claudio. (ed) *Dossier sul neofascismo a Trieste, 1945-1983*, Udine: Arti Grafiche Friulane, 1991.

Toynbee, Arnold. "Commentary," *New York Times Magazine*, November 3, 1963.

Troike, Muriel-Saville, "The Future of English," *The Linguistic Reporter*, Volume 19, Issue 8.

Turner, Bryan S. *Citizenship and Social Theory*, Sage Publications, 1993.

United Nations Development Programme. "Human Development   Report 2001 entitled some developing countries become high-tech leaders while others fall behind," July 10, 2001. Found at, http://www.undp.org/hdr2001.

United Nations Human Development Report of 2001. "Making New Technologies Work for Human Development," 2002.

United States Department of State. "Trends in the ICT Market," 2002.

United States English Foundation of Official Language Research.

Valarasan-Toomey, Mary. *The Celtic Tiger: From the OutsideLooking In*, Blackhall Publishing, 1998.

Valencic, Vida. "Slovene minority in Italy protest against neglection of Slovene language in census questionnaires," *Eurolang.net*, October 21, 2001. Found at: http://www.yeni.org/news/archives/00000025.htm.

Viswanathan, Gauri. *Masks of Conquest: Literary Study and British Rule in India*, Oxford University Press, 1998.

Vizmuller-Zocco, Jana. "The languages of Italian Canadians," *Italica*, Vol. 72, No. 4, Winter 1995, pp. 512-529.

Wagner, Cynthia. "Megacities of the future," *The Futurist*, Nov/Dec. 2001. Volume 35, Issue 6.

Walton, Nicholas. "Lemk people fight for survival," *BBC Online*, August 8, 2002.

War Department of the United States. "Acts of the PPhilippine Commission," from *Annual Reports of the War Department for the Fiscal Year Ended June 30,1902*, Volume 11. Washington: Government Printing Office, 1902. Accessed online: http://www.boondocksnet.com/centennial/sctexts/treason_act.html.

Weber, Max. Speech in Germany in 1918 entitled, "Gesammelte Politsche Schriften." Later published in *From Max Weber: Essays in Sociology*, by H.H. Gerth and C. Wright Mills (eds.). New York: NY, Oxford University Press, 1967.

Wigen, Karen. "Culture, Power, and Place: The New Landscape of East Asian Regionalism," *The American Historical Review*, vol. 104, no. 4, 1999, pp. 1183-1201.Wilenius, Markku. "A new globe in the making: Manuel Castells on the information Age," *Acta Sociologica*, Volume 41, Number 3, September 1, 1998, pp. 269-276.

Williams, Brendan J. "Italy and the Internet," April 15, 2001. From Webword.com. Accessed online at: http:// www.webword.com/moving/williams001.html

Witkowski, Wieslaw. "Commentaries" from the edited book of Paul Robert Magocsi entitled, *The Persistence of Regional Cultures*, 1993, pp. 187-190. Wood, David M. and Birol A. Yesilada. *The Emerging European Union*, Longman Publishing Group, 2001.

Woods, Ngaire. *Inequality, Globalization, and World Politics*, Oxford University Press, 1999.

Wriston, Walter B. *The Twilight of Sovereignty: How the Information Revolution is Transforming Our World*, Replica Books, 1997.

Ziac, Martin Fedor. "Professors and Politics: The Role of Paul Robert Paul Robert Magocsi in the Modern Carpatho-Rusyn Revival," *East European Quarterly*, XXXV, No. 2, June 2001.

Ziegler, J.N. "Corporate governance and the politics of property rights in Germany," *Oxford Review of Economic Policy*, Volume 16, Number 2, pp. 78-84, 2000.

Zimmern, Alfred (ed). *Modern Political Doctrines*. London, 1939.

Zulaika, Joseba and William Douglass. *Terror and Taboo: The Follies, Fables, and Faces of Terrorism*, Routledge Press, 1996.

Zurn, Michael. "The Challenge of Globalization and Individualization: A View from Europe," in Holm
and Sorenson (eds) *Whose World Order? Uneven Globalization and the End oft the Cold War*, pp 137-164.

Zysman, John. *Governments, Markets, and Growth: Financial Systems and the Politics of Industrial Change*, Oxford: Martin Robertson, 1983.

Lightning Source UK Ltd.
Milton Keynes UK
UKOW040835120512

192411UK00005B/31/P